MASTERING THE ART OF PROMPT ENGINEERING WITH ChatGPT

Tricks for Framing Killer Prompts in 2023

By :

Prabhakar Veeraraghavan

Mastering the Art of Prompt Engineering with ChatGPT

Tricks for framing killer prompts in 2023

By : Prabhakar Veeraraghavan

Copyright © 2023

by Prabhakar Veeraraghavan

Publication : Bilingual Publication

Type of book

Unlock the secrets of AI content generation with 'Mastering the Art of Prompt Engineering.' Learn cutting-edge techniques for harnessing ChatGPT's power in 2023. Level up your content creation game today!

About the author

Prabhakar Veeraraghavan is a Blogger and an accomplished Author after spending more than 2 decades in the corporate world. I am passionate in writing books with an innate ability to transport readers to captivating words and evoke profound emotions.

Combining remarkable creativity with meticulous attention to detail, my idea is to intricate plots that leave readers spellbound from the first page to the last. The motive is not to leave the reads just for the sake of reading but to involve them deep into the subject that have mind blowing effect upon completion of every book.

ALL RIGHTS RESERVED

A Word to the Readers and Writers

Welcome to "Mastering the Art of Prompt Engineering with ChatGPT." Tricks for framing Killer Prompts in 2023. It is with great excitement and anticipation that I present this e-book, a comprehensive guide designed to unravel the captivating world of **prompt engineering** in the realm of AI and natural language processing.

In the age of artificial intelligence, ChatGPT stands as a remarkable testament to the incredible advancements we've achieved in the field of technology. It is an AI language model, a virtual conversation partner, a creative collaborator, and a source of boundless knowledge. As we embark on this journey together, we will delve deep into the art and science of mastering prompt engineering, unlocking the full potential of ChatGPT and similar AI models.

The Power of Prompt Engineering

In order to truly appreciate the essence of prompt engineering, we must first understand its significance. The ability to communicate effectively with AI models is not just an emerging skill; it is the gateway to limitless possibilities. With well-constructed prompts, you can harness the power of AI to assist you in various domains – from generating creative content to solving complex problems and even extending the frontiers of human knowledge.

Each prompt is a carefully crafted key that opens doors to the vast reservoir of information residing within AI models like ChatGPT. And this e-book is your guide to crafting the perfect key.

A Journey of Learning and Discovery

This e-book is designed to cater to a diverse audience. Whether you're a student, a content creator, a professional in the field of AI, or simply an enthusiast eager to explore the world of AI language models, you'll find valuable insights and practical guidance within these pages.

The journey we're about to embark on will not be without its challenges. Prompt engineering is both an art and a science, a creative endeavour backed by a deep understanding of the underlying technologies. We will explore the principles that govern AI language models and, hand in hand, learn how to craft prompts that elicit the most informative, creative, and accurate responses.

What to Expect

In the chapters that follow, we'll begin with the basics: understanding AI language models and getting started with ChatGPT. We'll explore the syntax and semantics of language, discuss the intricacies of context and memory, and even uncover advanced techniques in prompt design.

You'll learn how to customize ChatGPT to your specific needs, optimizing content quality and ensuring ethical use. We'll dive into the metrics for evaluating AI-generated content, measuring success, and continuously refining your prompt engineering skills.

Case studies and real-world examples will provide a practical perspective, showing you how prompt engineering has been applied to diverse fields, from content generation to problem-solving.

I am sure no where you could find such an easy way of learning with tons of examples and prompts that a lay man can even understand from this book.

The Road Ahead

The journey through the art and science of mastering prompt engineering is a voyage of exploration, curiosity, and growth. As you read through these pages, I encourage you to embrace each concept, practice each technique, and ask questions.

Remember, the world of AI and prompt engineering is a dynamic one, and new horizons await your discovery. This e-book is not just a static guide but a catalyst for your journey. As you embark on this adventure, know that you are stepping into a world of endless possibilities, where your interaction with AI models like ChatGPT can be transformative and a game changer in building a strong profession that is going to dominate the next 3 decades of technological evolution.

Now, dear readers, I invite you to join me on this incredible voyage through the art and science of mastering prompt engineering. Let's embark on a journey of learning, creativity, and innovation that promises to reshape the way we interact with AI and unlock the untold potential of this remarkable technology.

May your exploration be filled with insights, your experiments yield wisdom, and your discoveries inspire others to explore the limitless realms of AI language models. Together, we'll master the Art and craft of prompt engineering, and together, we'll shape the future of human-AI collaboration.

Warmest regards and happy reading!!!

Table of Contents

Chapter 1: Introduction to Prompt Engineering

1.1 What is Prompt Engineering?

In the world of AI-driven content generation, prompt engineering is the secret sauce that transforms a mere string of text into a powerful directive for artificial intelligence models. It's the magic behind instructing machines to create content that aligns with your unique vision. Prompt engineering involves the careful crafting of instructions, queries, or prompts used to guide AI models in generating content.

Now let us put it in a lay man's language and understand what Prompt Engineering is ?

Prompt: Think of a prompt as a question or instruction that you give to a smart computer program, like ChatGPT. It's like asking a question to get a useful answer.

Engineering: Just like engineers build strong bridges or design cool gadgets, prompt engineering is about crafting and framing the best possible questions or instructions to get the answers exactly the way you want from the computer program.

So, it is clear that prompt engineering is the skill of asking computer programs the right questions or giving them the right instructions, like a wizard casting a spell, to make them give you the most helpful and accurate information or do specific tasks. It's like teaching a computer to be your super-smart helper!

To illustrate this concept, let's consider a practical example. Imagine you're tasked with generating a blog post on "**sustainable gardening tips**."

You could formulate a prompt like this: "**Generate a 1,000-word blog post on sustainable gardening practices, including tips on organic fertilizers and water conservation**." This prompt is your bridge to communicating your creative intent to an AI model.

Now ley us dive bit deeper into the concept of Prompt Engineering.

Imagine you have a magic genie, but instead of granting wishes, this genie can give you answers to questions or help you with tasks. This genie, in our real world, is a powerful computer program like ChatGPT. You can type in a question or tell it what you need, and it will do its best to provide you with a response.

Now, the thing is, this genie is really smart, but it's not human. It doesn't understand things the way we do. It follows a set of rules and patterns. So, if you want to get the best answers or results from it, you have to be a bit of a "**prompt engineer**."

Here's what that means:

Asking the Right Questions: When you ask your genie a question, you need to make sure you're asking it in a way it understands. If you're too vague or confusing, the genie might get mixed up and not give you the answer you want. So, prompt engineering is about figuring out how to phrase your questions clearly and precisely.

Giving Clear Instructions: Sometimes, you don't ask questions; you just tell the genie what you want it to do. Like saying, "Write a short story about a pirate adventure." To get the best story, you have to be good at giving clear instructions. That's part of prompt engineering, too.

Being Creative: The genie can be really creative, but it needs a bit of guidance. Prompt engineering involves thinking creatively about how you can ask your questions or give instructions to get unique, interesting, or useful responses.

Learning from Mistakes: It's like teaching a pet a new trick. Sometimes, you have to try different ways of asking or instructing until you get the result you're looking for. Prompt engineering involves experimenting and learning from what works and what doesn't.

Being Ethical: Just like we treat people with respect, we have to treat our genie with respect. Prompt engineering also means using the genie's powers responsibly and not asking it to do harmful or inappropriate things.

In a nutshell, prompt engineering is the skill of communicating effectively with your super-smart computer genie. It's about asking the right questions, giving clear instructions, being creative, learning from mistakes, and being a good digital citizen. It's a bit like having a conversation with a helpful but non-human friend who speaks a unique language, and you're learning to speak that language fluently.

1.2 Why is prompt engineering so crucial?

Customization: Effective prompt engineering allows you to customize the output of AI models. By using different prompts, you can guide the same AI model to generate content for a variety of purposes.

Content Control: It empowers you with control over the quality, tone, and style of the generated content. You can ensure the AI model produces content that adheres to your standards and brand voice.

Efficiency: Well-structured prompts save time and effort. Instead of laboriously crafting content from scratch, you can rely on prompt engineering to efficiently kickstart the content generation process.

Relevance: The precision of your prompts directly influences the relevance of the AI-generated output. A well-constructed prompt ensures that the content remains on-topic and aligned with your objectives.

Consistency: For brands and content platforms, consistent prompts enable the maintenance of a uniform style and voice across all content pieces, reinforcing brand identity.

1.3 The Role of Prompt Engineering in Content Generation

Prompt engineering serves as the linchpin for content generation with AI. It is the gatekeeper that ensures the AI-generated content aligns with your goals, requirements, and expectations. Let's delve into the key functions and roles of prompt engineering in content creation:

Creative Guidance: Prompt engineering provides creative direction to AI models, guiding them in understanding the type of content you wish to create. It sets the boundaries for the AI's creative expression.

Content Quality Control: Effective prompts act as quality control mechanisms. By specifying your expectations in prompts, you can ensure that the AI model generates content that meets your quality standards.

Adaptability: Prompts can be adapted to various content types and niches. Whether you need a scientific report, a persuasive marketing email, or a travel blog, prompt engineering allows you to tailor the AI's output to your specific needs.

Content Consistency: In the context of a brand or a content platform, consistent prompts help maintain a uniform style and tone across all content, reinforcing brand identity and audience expectations.

Efficiency and Productivity: Well-crafted prompts enhance productivity by streamlining content creation. Instead of starting from scratch, you can use prompts to initiate and direct the writing process, saving valuable time and resources.

1.4 Understanding the Power of AI in Content Creation

The capabilities of AI in content creation are nothing short of extraordinary. AI, driven by natural language processing (NLP) and machine learning, can generate content across a vast spectrum of genres and styles. The key to unlocking this potential lies in the structured prompts that AI models receive.

In this chapter, we'll explore the following aspects:

How AI Learns: An overview of how AI models are trained to understand and generate human-like text. We'll dive into the underlying neural networks, algorithms, and the concept of machine learning.

The Spectrum of NL: A look at the diverse range of content types that AI can create, from creative storytelling and persuasive marketing content to scientific reports and technical documentation.

Benefits of AI-Generated Content: We'll delve into the numerous advantages of AI content generation, including its speed, accuracy, scalability, and cost-efficiency.

AI in Practice: Real-world examples showcasing the power of AI in generating content. You'll witness how AI can produce high-quality, contextually relevant content on demand.

1.5 Examples of AI-Generated Content

To illustrate the potential of AI content generation, let's examine real-life examples of prompts and the content they generate:

Example 1: Product Descriptions

Prompt: "Create a product description for a stainless steel dishwasher."

AI-Generated Content: "Introducing our state-of-the-art stainless steel dishwasher, designed to make your daily chores a breeze. With its sleek design and advanced features, this dishwasher ensures sparkling clean dishes every time. Say goodbye to the hassle of handwashing and hello to convenience."

This example showcases how a well-structured prompt can result in a compelling product description that highlights key features and benefits.

Example 2: Blog Post Introduction

Prompt: "Write an engaging introduction for a blog post about 'Healthy Meal Prep Tips.'"

AI-Generated Content: "In today's fast-paced world, finding time to prepare healthy meals can be a challenge. But fear not, because we're about to embark on a culinary journey filled with time-saving tips and delicious recipes. Welcome to our guide on 'Healthy Meal Prep Tips.'"

Here, the prompt sets the tone for the blog post and provides a clear direction for the AI model to create an engaging introduction.

Example 3: Marketing Email Subject Line

Prompt: "Craft a subject line for a marketing email promoting a summer sale."

AI-Generated Content: " Unleash the Savings: Our Epic Summer Sale Is Here! "

The prompt efficiently instructs the AI model to create an attention-grabbing subject line with a summery feel, perfectly suited for a marketing email.

These examples demonstrate how well-crafted prompts are essential in achieving specific content goals, whether it's product descriptions, blog post introductions, or marketing email subject lines. By understanding the power of prompt engineering, you can unlock the potential of AI in content creation and elevate the quality of your output.

Chapter 2: The Fundamentals of AI and Natural Language Processing

2.1 Demystifying AI and Natural Language Processing (NLP)

In this chapter, we delve into the fundamental principles of AI and NLP, demystifying the technology that underpins prompt engineering and AI content generation.

The Essence of AI

Artificial Intelligence, or AI, is a multidisciplinary field of computer science that focuses on creating intelligent machines capable of performing tasks that typically require human intelligence. The core idea is to enable computers to think, learn, and make decisions in a way that mimics human intelligence.

At the heart of AI are algorithms, which are sets of rules or instructions that machines follow to achieve specific tasks. Machine learning is a subset of AI, where machines use data to learn and improve their performance over time.

Let's break down the fundamentals of AI (Artificial Intelligence) and Natural Language Processing (NLP) in simple terms.

AI is like teaching computers to be smart. Think of it as training a pet dog, but instead of fetching a ball, you're teaching the computer to understand and do human-like things, like answering questions, making decisions, or even being creative.

Now, here comes the NLP into the picture. NSP is a special part of AI that focuses on language. It's like teaching the computer to understand and speak human language, just like you and I. With NLP, computers can read, write, and talk to us. So, when you ask a voice assistant a question or type something into a search engine, NLP helps the computer understand what you mean and give you a useful answer. It's a bit like teaching your pet to understand and respond to your commands, but in this case, your "pet" is a computer that's really good with words!

Now let us see some examples of Training the pet (which is the computer) in getting the answer the way we want.

Example Prompt 1: "Explain the concept of machine learning in 200 words."

AI-Generated Content: "Machine learning is a subset of artificial intelligence that enables computers to learn from data and improve their performance without being explicitly programmed. It's like teaching a computer to make decisions based on patterns it recognizes in data. By analysing vast amounts of information, machine learning models can make predictions, classify data, and make recommendations. For example, in the world of e-commerce, machine learning helps suggest products to customers based on their browsing and buying history, ultimately enhancing the user experience."

Example Prompt 2: "Describe the difference between AI and machine learning."

AI-Generated Content: "AI and machine learning are often used interchangeably, but they have distinct differences. AI is the broader field, encompassing any technique that allows computers to mimic human intelligence. It includes machine learning, natural language processing, and expert systems, among other technologies. Machine learning, on the other hand, is a subset of AI focused on training algorithms to learn and make predictions from data. In summary, AI is the overarching concept, while machine learning is a specific technique within that concept."

Natural Language Processing (NLP)

NLP is a branch of AI that deals with the interaction between computers and humans through natural language. It enables computers to understand, interpret, and generate human language in a way that is both valuable and meaningful.

Example Prompt 3: "Explain the core components of NLP."

AI-Generated Content: "Natural Language Processing (NLP) is a multidisciplinary field at the intersection of computer science, artificial intelligence, and linguistics. It involves three core components:

Language Understanding: NLP models must be able to understand the structure and meaning of language. This includes tasks like part-of-speech tagging and named entity recognition.

Language Generation: NLP enables machines to generate human-like language. This is particularly important in tasks like text generation and chatbot responses.

Language Translation: NLP allows for language translation, making it possible for machines to convert text from one language to another, enabling global communication and accessibility."

Example Prompt 4: "Provide an example of a real-world NLP application."

AI-Generated Content: "One of the most prominent real-world applications of NLP is machine translation. Google Translate, for instance, uses NLP algorithms to translate text from one language to another. It works by analysing the input text's structure, syntax, and semantics and generating an equivalent text in the desired language. This has revolutionized cross-cultural communication, making information and resources accessible to people worldwide."

2.2 Tokenization and Text Preprocessing of NLP

In Natural Language Processing (NLP), tokenization and text processing are fundamental techniques for understanding and working with human language.

Tokenization: Tokenization is like chopping up a paragraph or a sentence into smaller pieces, kind of like breaking a long piece of text into individual words. These smaller pieces are called "tokens." Tokenization helps a computer understand where one word ends and the next one starts. It's a bit like separating beads on a necklace, so you can see each bead on its own. This is crucial because it enables the computer to process and analyze text more effectively, like counting words or checking for patterns.

Text Processing: Once you have these tokens, text processing is the next step. It's like arranging those separated words or tokens to make sense of them. You might want to correct typos, remove unnecessary words, or figure out the most important words in a text. Text processing helps the computer understand the meaning of the words and how they relate to each other. It's like organizing those beads from the necklace into a beautiful pattern or piece of jewellery. Text processing allows the computer to perform tasks like translation, sentiment analysis, or summarizing text, making it a valuable part of NLP.

Now let's put "tokenization" and "text processing" in simple terms.

Tokenization: Imagine you have a big box of words, like a puzzle with lots of pieces. Tokenization is like breaking this puzzle into smaller, individual pieces. Each piece is one word or a small chunk of words. So, instead of dealing with the whole puzzle at once, you're looking at each piece separately. It makes it easier for a computer to understand and work with the words in a sentence.

Text Processing: Now, think of text processing as making sense of these word pieces. It's like putting the pieces back together in a way that's helpful. You might want to organize them, correct spelling mistakes, or count how many times a word appears.

Text processing is all about getting the words in your puzzle to work together, so you can do things like search for information or understand what a text is about. It's like turning a jumble of puzzle pieces into a clear picture.

2.3 Key Terminology in NLP

To navigate the world of NLP effectively, it's crucial to understand some key terminology.

1. Corpus

A corpus is a collection of text documents used for linguistic research and analysis. Corpora (plural of corpus) serve as the foundation for training NLP models and developing language understanding.

Example Prompt 5: "Define what a corpus is in the context of NLP."

AI-Generated Content: "In the field of natural language processing (NLP), a corpus refers to a structured collection of text documents or linguistic data. Corpora are essential for various NLP tasks, such as training machine learning models, conducting linguistic research, and building language models. They enable the analysis of language patterns, the extraction of linguistic insights, and the development of language understanding."

2. Tokenization

Tokenization is the process of dividing a text into smaller units, such as words or phrases, to facilitate analysis. In NLP, tokens are typically words or subworlds.

Example Prompt 6: "Explain the concept of tokenization and its significance in NLP."

AI-Generated Content: "Tokenization is a fundamental process in natural language processing (NLP) that involves breaking down a text into smaller units, known as tokens. These tokens can be words, subwords, or even characters, depending on the level of granularity required for analysis. Tokenization is crucial in NLP because it allows machines to process and understand human language, making it easier to extract meaning, perform language analysis, and train language models."

3. Part-of-Speech Tagging

Part-of-speech tagging involves labelling each word in a text with its corresponding part of speech, such as nouns, verbs, adjectives, and adverbs.

Example Prompt 7: "Describe the purpose of part-of-speech tagging in NLP."

AI-Generated Content: "Part-of-speech tagging is a vital task in natural language processing (NLP) that aims to label each word in a text with its appropriate part of speech. This process allows NLP models to understand the grammatical structure of sentences, enabling tasks such as syntactic analysis, sentiment analysis, and named entity recognition. By assigning parts of speech to words, NLP models can extract information about the relationships and roles of words within a sentence, contributing to a deeper understanding of the text."

4. Named Entity Recognition (NER)

Named Entity Recognition (NER) is the process of identifying and categorizing named entities in text, such as names of people, places, organizations, and dates.

Example Prompt 8:** "Explain the significance of Named Entity Recognition (NER) in NLP."

AI-Generated Content: "Named Entity Recognition (NER) is a crucial NLP task that involves identifying and categorizing named entities in text. NER plays a pivotal role in various applications, including information retrieval, question-answering systems, and text summarization. By recognizing and categorizing entities like names of people, places, organizations, and dates, NER allows NLP models to extract valuable information and improve text understanding. This is particularly valuable in applications that require the extraction of specific facts and details from unstructured text."

2.4 Practical NLP Applications

NLP is a versatile field with applications spanning various domains. Let's explore some practical NLP applications and their significance.

1. Sentiment Analysis

Sentiment analysis, also known as opinion mining, is the process of determining the sentiment or emotional tone expressed in a piece of text, such as positive, negative, or neutral.

Example Prompt 9: "Explain the concept of sentiment analysis and its real-world applications."

AI-Generated Content: "Sentiment analysis, a prominent NLP application, involves the automated assessment of sentiment or emotion expressed in text. This technology is used in various real-world applications, including social media monitoring, customer feedback analysis, and market research. For instance, businesses use sentiment analysis to gauge public opinion about their products or services, helping them make.

2.5 Syntax and Semantics in Natural Language Processing (NLP)

In the field of Natural Language Processing (NLP), two critical aspects play a fundamental role in understanding and processing human language: syntax and semantics. These aspects are central to enabling machines to comprehend and generate human language effectively. This chapter explores the significance of syntax and semantics in NLP, their key differences, and their practical applications.

Understanding Syntax

Syntax refers to the structure and rules governing the arrangement of words in a language to create well-formed sentences. It deals with the relationship between words, phrases, and clauses and how they are combined to convey meaning. Syntax provides the framework for organizing language, ensuring that sentences are grammatically correct and coherent.

Key Aspects of Syntax:

Word Order: Different languages have distinct word orders, such as subject-verb-object (SVO) in English or subject-object-verb (SOV) in Japanese. Syntax dictates the permissible word orders within a language.

Grammatical Rules: Every language has its set of grammatical rules. Syntax determines how sentences are formed, including rules for verb conjugation, tense, and agreement.

Dependency Parsing: In NLP, dependency parsing is used to identify the grammatical relationships between words in a sentence. This parsing technique helps determine which words depend on others for meaning.

Syntax Trees: A syntax tree (or parse tree) is a visual representation of the grammatical structure of a sentence, breaking it down into its constituent parts.

Example:

In English, the sentence "The quick brown fox jumps over the lazy dog" follows a specific word order (subject-verb-object). Syntax governs the correct arrangement of words in this sentence to convey its intended meaning.

Understanding Semantics

Semantics delves into the meaning of words, phrases, and sentences. It is concerned with how words are used to convey information, the relationships between words, and how meaning is inferred from language. Semantics goes beyond the grammatical structure to explore the deeper layers of significance in language.

Key Aspects of Semantics:

Word Meaning: Semantics examines the meaning of individual words, including their definitions, connotations, and denotations. It distinguishes between literal and figurative meanings.

Word Sense Disambiguation: Many words have multiple meanings depending on the context. Semantics helps in determining the correct sense of a word in a particular context.

Semantic Role Labelling: This process assigns specific roles to words within a sentence, such as identifying the agent, patient, or theme in a verb's action.

Pragmatics: While semantics deals with the literal meaning of words, pragmatics focuses on the implied meaning, considering factors like context, tone, and speaker intention.

Ontologies and Knowledge Representation: In NLP, ontologies and knowledge graphs are used to represent and link concepts, enhancing the understanding of semantic relationships.

Example:

Consider the word "bark." In the sentence "The dog's bark is loud," the word "bark" refers to the sound a dog makes. In contrast, in the sentence "The tree has rough bark," "bark" refers to the protective outer covering of a tree. Understanding the different semantic senses of "bark" is vital for accurate comprehension.

Syntactic and Semantic Analysis in NLP

In NLP, both syntax and semantics are crucial for tasks like language understanding, generation, and machine translation.

Semantic Analysis:

Extracting the meaning and context of words and sentences.

Semantic analysis is used in tasks such as sentiment analysis, named entity recognition, and information retrieval.

Practical Applications

Understanding syntax and semantics in NLP has a wide range of practical applications:

Machine Translation: Accurate translation between languages requires both syntactic and semantic analysis to convey the meaning of sentences correctly.

Information Retrieval: Search engines use semantic analysis to understand user queries and retrieve relevant documents.

Sentiment Analysis: Determining the sentiment or emotional tone of a text relies on semantic analysis to identify positive, negative, or neutral sentiments.

Speech Recognition: In speech-to-text applications, both syntax and semantics help in accurately transcribing spoken language.

Question Answering Systems: Semantic analysis aids in understanding and retrieving answers from text based on the meaning of the question.

In conclusion, syntax and semantics are two foundational pillars in the field of Natural Language Processing. Syntax governs the structure and grammatical correctness of language, while semantics delves into the meaning and interpretation of words and sentences. The interplay between these two aspects is crucial for enabling machines to understand, generate, and interact with human language effectively.

Chapter 3: Crafting Effective Prompts

3.1 What Makes a Good Prompt?

In this chapter, we will dive into the art and science of crafting effective prompts for AI content generation. A well-structured prompt is the key to obtaining the desired output from AI models. Let's start by understanding the elements that make a prompt effective.

Clarity and Specificity

An effective prompt must be clear and specific in its instruction. Vague or ambiguous prompts can lead to unpredictable results. When crafting a prompt, consider the following:

Example Prompt 1: "Write an article on climate change."

AI-Generated Content: The AI model might generate a general article about climate change as what is climate change, but it won't address specific aspects or angles related to the topic.

Effective Prompt: "Compose a 1,000-word article discussing the impact of rising sea levels on coastal communities due to climate change, and suggest adaptation strategies."

AI-Generated Content: With this specific prompt, the AI model will focus on the impact of rising sea levels on coastal communities, providing a more in-depth and targeted article. Are you able to find the difference in giving "attention to detail" by AI in producing this output. The detail information is "**To point out the impact of rising sea levels on coastal communities because of the climate change**".

Tone and Style

The tone and style of a prompt should align with the desired content. Whether you need a formal research report or a casual blog post, your prompt should reflect the appropriate tone and style.

Example Prompt 2: "Write a blog post about space exploration."

AI-Generated Content: The AI model could produce a blog post with an unspecified tone, making it challenging to predict the style and audience.

pg. 43

Whereas see this effective Prompt below :

Effective Prompt: "Create a 700-word blog post in an engaging and informative style, highlighting recent breakthroughs in space exploration and their potential impact on future missions."

AI-Generated Content: With this prompt, no doubt the AI model will understand the need for an engaging style and focus on recent space exploration breakthroughs, resulting in content that aligns with the desired tone and style. The more clarity and search terms you feed in the more attention to detailed output you will get from AI.

Inclusion of Keywords

Including specific keywords in your prompt can help ensure that the AI-generated content is optimized for search engines (SEO) or targets particular topics.

Example Prompt 3: "Write a product description for a smartwatch."

AI-Generated Content: Without specific keywords, the AI model may create a generic product description.

Effective Prompt: "Craft a product description for a smartwatch with a focus on features like fitness tracking, heart rate monitoring, and smartphone compatibility."

AI-Generated Content: Including keywords like "fitness tracking" and "heart rate monitoring" guides the AI to emphasize those features, resulting in a more tailored product description.

3.2 Tips for Constructing Effective Prompts

Creating effective prompts requires attention to detail and careful consideration. Here are some valuable tips for constructing prompts that yield the best results:

1. Be Specific

Specificity is paramount. Clearly define what you want the AI to produce. The more specific your instructions, the more likely you are to receive content that meets your expectations.

Example Prompt 4: "Write a product review."

AI-Generated Content: Without specific details, the AI model may struggle to determine what product to review and what aspects to cover.

Effective Prompt: "Write a 500-word review of the iPhone 13, focusing on its camera capabilities, performance, and battery life."

AI-Generated Content: This specific prompt obviously guides the AI model to create a targeted review of the iPhone 13, covering the designated aspects.

2. Use Action Verbs

Incorporate action verbs to convey a clear task. Action verbs provide a strong directive to the AI model, reducing ambiguity.

Example Prompt 5: "Discuss the advantages of renewable energy."

AI-Generated Content: The prompt lacks a clear task, and the AI model may produce a broad overview.

Effective Prompt: "Summarize the economic benefits of renewable energy in a 500-word article, focusing on job creation and reduced energy costs."

AI-Generated Content: With an action verb ("summarize") and specific focus ("job creation" and "reduced energy costs"), the AI model receives a clear directive.

3. Include Context

Providing context helps the AI understand the purpose and audience of the content. Explain why the content is needed and who it is intended for.

Example Prompt 6: "Write an article about electric cars."

AI-Generated Content: Without context, the AI model may produce a generic article with no specific angle.

Effective Prompt: "Create a 700-word article aimed at consumers interested in purchasing their first electric car. Provide an overview of key benefits, charging options, and cost considerations."

AI-Generated Content: The inclusion of context ("aimed at consumers interested in purchasing their first electric car") helps the AI model tailor the content to a specific audience.

4. Set Length and Structure

Specify the desired length of the content and, if necessary, provide a suggested structure or format. This ensures that the AI generates content that fits your requirements.

Example Prompt 7: "Write a blog post about healthy eating."

AI-Generated Content: Without length and structure guidance, the AI model might produce a blog post that varies in length and structure.

Effective Prompt: "Compose a 1,000-word blog post with the following structure: Introduction, Benefits of Healthy Eating, Practical Tips, and Conclusion."

AI-Generated Content: With a clearly defined length and structure, the AI model will create content that adheres to the specified format and the number of words that you require, even though it may not be the exact number of words.

3.3 Real-World Examples of Prompts

To further illustrate the concepts discussed, let's examine real-world examples of prompts and the resulting AI-generated content.

Example Prompt 8: "Write a product description for a laptop."

AI-Generated Content: The AI model may create a generic laptop description with no specific focus.

Effective Prompt: "Craft a product description for a 14-inch Ultrabook laptop, emphasizing its lightweight design, long battery life, and suitability for business professionals on the go."

AI-Generated Content: With this specific prompt, the AI model produces a product description tailored to the features that matter most to the target audience.

Example Prompt 9: "Write an email marketing campaign."

AI-Generated Content: Without further details, the AI model might generate a general email marketing campaign.

Effective Prompt: "Develop a series of three email marketing messages for a fitness apparel brand's summer sale. The first email should announce the sale, the second should highlight popular products, and the third should create urgency by mentioning the limited-time offer."

AI-Generated Content: With a structured prompt, the AI model creates a coherent email marketing campaign aligned with the brand's objectives.

Example Prompt 10: "Create a social media post."

AI-Generated Content: The AI model may produce a vague social media post with no clear purpose or message.

Effective Prompt: "Generate a social media post to promote a charity run event. The post should include an engaging call to action, event details, and a compelling image related to running."

AI-Generated Content: This structured prompt ensures that the AI generates a social media post tailored to the charity run event, including all essential elements for promotion.

3.4 The importance of clarity and Specificity.

Crafting Clear and Specific Prompts

In the realm of AI content generation, the quality of the prompt is paramount. Clarity and specificity within prompts are not just desirable attributes; they are fundamental prerequisites for achieving the desired output from AI models. This chapter underscores the significance of crafting prompts that are clear, explicit, and meticulously tailored to your content objectives.

Clarity: The Keystone of Effective Prompts

Clarity within a prompt refers to its capacity to convey a clear and unambiguous message to the AI model. Think of clarity as the language through which you and the AI communicate. Unclear or convoluted prompts can lead to misunderstandings, resulting in content that deviates from your intended goal.

Example of an Unclear Prompt:

"Write about renewable energy in a way that's engaging but not too technical."

In the above example, the prompt lacks clarity. It uses terms like "engaging" and "not too technical" without defining what those terms mean in the context of the content. This could lead to varied interpretations and, consequently, a less predictable outcome.

Example of a Clear Prompt:

"Create a 700-word blog post that introduces the concept of renewable energy to a general audience. Avoid technical jargon and use relatable examples to illustrate key points."

This revised prompt offers explicit instructions, defining the content's length, target audience, and tone. It provides a clear roadmap for the AI model to follow, ensuring that the resulting content aligns with your intentions.

Specificity: The North Star of Effective Prompts

Specificity in prompts refers to the level of detail and precision in the instruction. The more specific a prompt, the more control you exert over the content generated. Specific prompts minimize the risk of misinterpretation and ensure that the AI model focuses on the aspects you deem most important.

Example of a Non-Specific Prompt:

"Write an article about smartphones."

This prompt is overly broad and lacks specificity. Without further details, it's unclear what aspects of smartphones the article should cover. The AI model might produce content on smartphone history, technical specifications, or market trends, making it challenging to predict the outcome.

Example of a Specific Prompt:

"Compose a 1,000-word article comparing the camera features of the latest iPhone and Android smartphones. Include details about camera hardware, software enhancements, and real-world photography examples."

In this specific prompt, you've defined the article's length, topic, and key focus areas. The AI model receives clear guidance on what to include in the content, resulting in a well-structured, information-rich article.

The Consequences of Unclear and Non-Specific Prompts

The consequences of crafting prompts that lack clarity and specificity can be detrimental to your content generation process:

Inconsistent Output: Unclear or non-specific prompts can lead to inconsistent content output. The AI model might generate content that varies widely in style, depth, or relevance to the topic.

Time and Resource Wastage: A lack of specificity in prompts can result in content that doesn't meet your needs. This necessitates additional time and effort to review, revise, or rewrite the content, which can be resource-intensive.

Misalignment with Objectives: Unclear prompts can result in content that doesn't align with your content objectives, causing frustration and hindering your goals.

Missed Opportunities: Non-specific prompts may miss opportunities for the AI model to create highly relevant and valuable content that addresses the specific angles, questions, or details you intended.

How to Enhance Clarity and Specificity in Prompts

To harness the full potential of AI in content generation, it's crucial to enhance the clarity and specificity of your prompts. Here are some practical strategies to achieve this:

1. Define the Objective

Begin by clearly defining the objective of the content you wish to create. What is the purpose of the content, and what do you want to achieve with it? This clarity provides a strong foundation for crafting a precise prompt.

Example:

Objective: "Create a product description that highlights the key features of a new smartphone model to attract potential buyers."

2. Identify the Target Audience

Understand your target audience, their preferences, and their level of expertise on the topic. This knowledge informs the tone, style, and level of detail in your prompt.

Example:

Target Audience: "Tech-savvy consumers interested in purchasing the latest smartphone."

3. Specify Content Parameters

Clearly specify essential parameters, such as content length, structure, and any specific elements you want to include in the content.

Example:

Content Parameters: "Craft a 500-word blog post with an introduction, three main points, and a conclusion. Include statistics and user testimonials to support the key points."

4. Avoid Ambiguity

Eliminate ambiguity from your prompts. Be cautious of vague terms, such as "engaging," "informative," or "unique." Instead, define precisely what you mean by these terms.

Example:

Ambiguous Term: "Create an engaging blog post."

Revised for Clarity: "Produce a 700-word blog post that engages readers by sharing real-life success stories related to sustainable living."

5. Use Action Verbs

Incorporate action verbs that convey a clear task or action the AI model should perform. Action verbs provide strong, direct instructions.

Example:

Non-Specific Prompt: "Write about eco-friendly practices."

Revised with Action Verb: "Compose a 1,000-word article detailing five actionable eco-friendly practices for daily life."

6. Provide Examples or Models

Including examples or models within your prompt can clarify your expectations and guide the AI model in content creation.

Example:

Example-Enhanced Prompt: "Craft a product description similar to this one for Product X: 'Product X is a versatile tool designed to streamline your daily tasks. With its user-friendly interface and powerful features, it's the perfect companion for productivity.'"

7. Review and Revise

Before finalizing a prompt, review it for clarity and specificity. Put yourself in the shoes of the AI model and consider whether the prompt provides all the information needed to create the desired content.

Chapter 4: Leveraging Pretrained Models in AI Content Generation

4.1 Introduction to Pretrained Models

In the dynamic world of AI content generation, pretrained models stand as a testament to the power of machine learning and natural language processing. These models are not just algorithms; they are sophisticated neural networks trained on vast corpora of text data, designed to understand and generate human-like language.

To put it in simple terms, think of a pre-trained model like a very clever student who has already learned a lot of things. This student has read tons of books, practiced lots of problems, and knows a whole bunch about a specific subject, like math, science, or even how to write stories.

Now, when you want to solve a problem or write an essay, you can ask this clever student for help. Instead of starting from scratch, the student already has a head start because they've learned so much. So, you ask your question or give your topic, and the student gives you a really good answer or writes a great essay. It's like having a super-smart study buddy who has all the knowledge you need, and you can use their knowledge to get your work done faster and better. That's what a pre-trained model in AI is like—it's a clever, well-learned assistant that's ready to help you with all sorts of tasks.

In this chapter, we'll embark on a journey to explore the realm of pretrained models, understanding their significance, and how to effectively harness their capabilities.

4.2 Pros and Cons of Pretrained Models

The Pros

Pretrained models are revolutionizing AI content generation for several compelling reasons:

Language Understanding: Pretrained models possess a deep understanding of human language, enabling them to generate content that is contextually relevant and coherent, which is easy to understand. They excel in understanding nuances and idiomatic expressions, producing text that sounds remarkably as human.

Adaptability: These models are adaptable to a wide range of domains and content types. Whether it's creating marketing copy, generating code, or crafting poetry, pretrained models can be fine-tuned to excel in various tasks. It is like a student learning all the subjects of a class and answering the questions in a flash of a second.

Multilingual Competence: Many pretrained models are proficient in multiple languages, making them invaluable for businesses and individuals looking to expand their global reach.

Efficiency: Pretrained models can expedite the content creation process. They have the ability to produce high-quality content at scale, saving both time and effort, subject to ethical usage of the prompt and the content.

Natural Language Generation: These models excel in generating human-like text, which is crucial for applications like chatbots, virtual assistants, and automated customer support that can replace human presence both onsite and offsite (remote working) in replying to queries.

The Cons

While pretrained models offer substantial benefits, it's crucial to be aware of their limitations and potential drawbacks: Lets analyse them one by one below :

1. **Data Dependency**: These models heavily rely on the quality and quantity of training data. In cases where the training data is biased or unrepresentative, the generated content may reflect those biases.

2. **Lack of Real-World Knowledge**: Pretrained models do not possess real-world knowledge or common sense. They generate text based on patterns and information in their training data, which means they may provide incorrect or nonsensical information. This is more so in case of certain niches like current affairs, News Rooms, Education and Health.

3. **Ethical Concerns:** The use of pretrained models can raise ethical concerns, such as the generation of fake news, misinformation, or biased content. Careful oversight is necessary to ensure responsible use.

4.3 Choosing the Right Model for Your Needs

Selecting the right pretrained model for your content generation needs is essential. Here are some considerations to keep in mind:

Task Specificity: Determine the specific task or application for which you need the model. Some pretrained models are designed for general content generation, while others are fine-tuned for more specific tasks, like translation or summarization.

Language Support: If you require content in multiple languages, choose a model that supports the languages you need.

Training Data Quality: Research the training data used for a model. Models trained on diverse and high-quality data tend to perform better and generate less biased content.

Fine-Tuning: If your project necessitates fine-tuning the model for a specific task, make sure the chosen model is amenable to customization.

Ethical Considerations: Be aware of the ethical implications of your content generation. Choose models that prioritize ethical content generation, and monitor their output for potential biases or harmful content.

4.4 Demonstrations with GPT-3

To illustrate the power of pretrained models, let's explore some practical demonstrations using OpenAI's GPT-3.

Demonstration 1: Creative Writing

Prompt: "Write a short story about a scientist who discovers a parallel universe."

GPT-3 Output: "Dr. Samantha Edwards had always been obsessed with the idea of parallel universes. Her late-night experiments in the basement lab had finally paid off. As she stepped through the shimmering portal, she found herself in a world where everything was the same, yet different. The possibilities were endless."

Demonstration 2: Content Summarization

Prompt: "Summarize the key findings of the IPCC report on climate change."

GPT-3 Output: "The latest IPCC report highlights the dire consequences of climate change. It emphasizes rising global temperatures, extreme weather events, and the urgent need for immediate action to reduce greenhouse gas emissions and transition to renewable energy sources."

Demonstration 3: Language Translation

Prompt: "Translate the following English text to French: 'The Eiffel Tower is an iconic symbol of France.'"

GPT-3 Output: "La Tour Eiffel est un symbole emblématique de la France."

Demonstration 4: Generating Marketing Copy

Prompt: "Write a product description for a high-end smartphone with a focus on camera quality and performance."

GPT-3 Output: "Introducing the latest smartphone, designed for photography enthusiasts and power users. Capture stunning photos and videos with its state-of-the-art camera, while enjoying blazing-fast performance for all your apps and games."

Demonstration 5: Code Generation

Prompt: "Generate Python code to calculate the Fibonacci sequence."

GPT-3 Output:

python

```python
def fibonacci(n):

    if n <= 0:

        return []

    elif n == 1:

        return [0]

    elif n == 2:

        return [0, 1]

    else:

        fib = [0, 1]

        for i in range(2, n):

            fib.append(fib[i-1] + fib[i-2])

        return fib
```

python

These demonstrations showcase the versatility and capabilities of pretrained models like GPT-3. They can be harnessed for creative writing, content summarization, language translation, marketing copy generation, and even code development.

Related Resource : For those who are Code developers and Non Coders as well, you can always leverage the art of coding from a related resource that specializes on Coding prompts.   Just visit https://bard.google.com and leverage the potential of AI in getting the coding done in minutes.

Chapter 5: Fine-Tuning Models for Your Needs

5.1 Customizing Pretrained Models

In the world of AI content generation, the ability to customize pretrained models is a game-changer. Fine-tuning models allows you to tailor them to your specific needs, enabling the generation of content that aligns with your objectives. This chapter delves into the concept of fine-tuning, its importance, the process involved, and real-life case studies that showcase its transformative potential.

To put it in simple terms, Imagine you have a robot that's pretty smart and knows how to do lots of things. It can clean, cook, and even play music. But, here's the cool part: you can teach it to do things your way.

Customizing a pretrained model is like teaching your robot new tricks. You're telling it, "Hey, when you make my morning coffee, add a little extra cream and sugar, just how I like it." Or, "Play my favourite song when I walk in the door."

So, instead of using the robot's default settings, you're making it work just the way you want. You're personalizing it to fit your needs perfectly. Customizing a pretrained model in AI is like having a robot assistant that's not only smart but also tailored to your preferences.

5.2 The Process of Fine-Tuning

Fine-tuning is the process of training a pretrained model on a more specific dataset or for a particular task. It involves exposing the model to new data that is relevant to your content generation goals. The aim is to make the model adapt and specialize, refining its performance in areas that matter most to you.

Key Steps in the Fine-Tuning Process

Data Collection: Gather a dataset that is tailored to your task. This dataset should include examples that cover the specific content you want the model to generate.

Model Selection: Choose the pretrained model that serves as the foundation for fine-tuning. This choice depends on the language, domain, and structure of your content.

Hyperparameter Tuning: Adjust hyperparameters like learning rates, batch sizes, and training steps to optimize the model's performance for your task.

Fine-Tuning: Train the model on your task-specific dataset. This step fine-tunes the model's weights and biases to make it more proficient in generating the type of content you require.

Evaluation: Assess the fine-tuned model's performance through metrics or human evaluation. This step helps determine if the model meets your content generation objectives.

Iterative Refinement: Fine-tuning is often an iterative process. You may need to repeat the process, adjusting hyperparameters and expanding the dataset as needed to enhance the model's performance.

5.3 Real-Life Case Studies

Fine-tuning pretrained models has led to remarkable achievements in various industries. Here are some real-life case studies that exemplify its potential:

Case Study 1: Medical Content Generation

Objective: Generate medical reports from radiological images, automating the process of report creation and improving the efficiency of healthcare services.

Fine-Tuning: A pretrained model was fine-tuned on a dataset of radiological images and corresponding reports. The model learned to analyse images and generate detailed medical reports based on visual data.

Results: The fine-tuned model significantly reduced the time required to produce medical reports. It improved the accuracy of diagnoses and reduced the burden on radiologists, leading to faster healthcare delivery and better patient outcomes.

Case Study 2: Legal Document Generation

Objective: Automate the creation of legal documents, such as contracts and agreements, to save time and reduce errors in legal content.

Fine-Tuning: A pretrained language model was fine-tuned on a corpus of legal documents and their variations. The model learned to understand legal terminology, structure, and clauses.

Results: The fine-tuned model streamlined the process of generating legal documents. It provided accurate and legally sound content, reducing the risk of errors and ensuring compliance with legal standards.

Case Study 3: Content Moderation

Objective: Enhance content moderation on online platforms to identify and remove harmful or inappropriate content.

Fine-Tuning: A pretrained model was fine-tuned on a dataset of offensive or harmful content, teaching it to recognize patterns and context associated with problematic language and imagery.

Results: The fine-tuned model improved the accuracy of content moderation, reducing the presence of harmful content on online platforms. It minimized the exposure of users to inappropriate material and created safer online environments.

Case Study 4: E-Commerce Product Descriptions

Objective: Generate product descriptions for an e-commerce website that are both informative and engaging, driving sales and improving the shopping experience.

Fine-Tuning: A pretrained model was fine-tuned on a dataset of e-commerce product descriptions and their corresponding performance metrics. The model learned to craft persuasive and informative descriptions.

Results: The fine-tuned model created product descriptions that were not only accurate but also compelling. This led to increased user engagement, longer time spent on product pages, and higher conversion rates.

5.4 Ensuring Ethical Use of AI Models

As the power of fine-tuned AI models grows, so does the responsibility to use them ethically. Here are some essential considerations to ensure ethical usage:

Bias Mitigation: Be vigilant about potential biases in the fine-tuned model. Regularly assess and address biases to prevent the generation of harmful or discriminatory content. Since you are fine tuning Ai to meet your needs, be sure not to customize wrong content or method to analyse and produce the output, for it may lead to a disastrous situation.

Content Review: Implement a review process for content generated by AI models. Human oversight can catch errors and ensure that the content aligns with your ethical standards.

Clear Guidelines: Establish clear guidelines and standards for the use of AI-generated content. Ensure that everyone involved understands these guidelines and follows them without surpassing the recommended protocols of using AI generated content.

Transparency: Be transparent with your audience about the use of AI-generated content. If users are interacting with AI-driven chatbots or reading AI-generated articles, make it clear that the content is machine-generated.

Regular Updates: AI models should be continuously updated and refined to improve their ethical performance. Stay informed about model updates and integrate them into your workflow. Don't be outdated with the information or lack of correct information in the related topics.

User Feedback: Encourage users to provide feedback on AI-generated content. Their insights can help identify and rectify issues and to constantly improve your customization part thereby standing by the for the crowd who only make the Model a successful one.

Remember, the level of customization depends on the complexity of your task and the model you're using. Some tasks may require more extensive customization, while others can be achieved with minor adjustments. Customizing pre-trained models empowers you to use AI in a way that suits your unique needs and goals.

5.5 Testing and Validating Fine Tune Models

Testing and validating is a crucial step in customizing pre-trained models. It's like checking and confirming that your customized model works the way you want it to. Here's a more detailed explanation:

Testing: Think of this as trying out your customized model. You give it some input or a task, and you see what it does. For instance, if you're using a language model to write articles, you might ask it to write a sample article. The testing phase is like watching the robot perform a new trick you taught it.

Validation: Validation is a bit like double-checking. After the model has generated something or completed a task, you want to make sure it did it right. So, you review the output carefully to see if it meets your expectations. It's like tasting the food your robot chef prepared to ensure it's delicious.

Fine-Tuning: If the model's output isn't perfect, you might need to fine-tune it some more, like giving your robot additional lessons to improve its skills. You can adjust the training data, parameters, or feedback based on the testing and validation results.

Quality Assurance Just as food needs to meet certain standards to be served, the output of your model needs to meet certain quality criteria. This could involve checking for accuracy, clarity, or appropriateness, depending on your task.

Iterate: If you find that the model isn't consistently performing as expected, you may need to go back and iterate the process. Make adjustments, retest, validate, and keep refining until the results are consistently good.

In essence, testing and validating ensure that your customized model is reliable, accurate, and aligned with your specific goals. It's like making sure your trained dog can perform a new trick flawlessly every time you ask, and if not, you provide more training until it gets it right.

Chapter 6: Advanced Prompt Strategies

6.1 Advanced Techniques for Prompt Engineering

The art of prompt engineering has evolved to encompass advanced techniques that leverage the full potential of AI models for content generation. In this chapter, we will explore these techniques and how they can be harnessed to create content that is not only contextually relevant but also more engaging and effective.

Advanced techniques of prompt engineering involve taking your interactions with AI models to the next level. It's like having a deep conversation with a friend rather than just exchanging pleasantries. One key advanced technique is mastering the art of context and memory. It's about creating prompts that consider what you've previously discussed with the AI model, so your conversation flows naturally, just like a great chat with a knowledgeable friend who remembers what you talked about last time. This leads to richer, more in-depth responses.

Another advanced technique is using specialized prompts. It's like asking your AI model for assistance in a way that's tailor-made for a specific task. For instance, if you're a content creator, you might use prompts that guide the AI to brainstorm ideas, outline articles, or even craft catchy headlines. These prompts act like providing detailed instructions, ensuring you get the exact kind of help you need. It's like having a personal assistant who knows your work preferences and can support you effectively. By incorporating these advanced techniques, you can unlock the full potential of prompt engineering, making your interactions with AI models more precise, insightful, and productive.

Prompt Engineering: A Recap

Prompt engineering is the process of crafting instructions or queries that guide AI models in generating specific content. It serves as the bridge between your requirements and the AI's capabilities. Effective prompt engineering ensures that the AI understands your objectives and produces content that aligns with them.

Advanced Techniques

Multi-Step Prompts: Multi-step prompts involve breaking down complex tasks into a series of sub-tasks. By providing the AI with step-by-step instructions, you can generate intricate and detailed content.

Example: Instead of asking for a single product description, you can use a multi-step prompt to instruct the AI to provide a headline, list key features, and create a compelling closing statement for the product.

Conditional Prompts: Conditional prompts allow you to steer the AI's output based on specific criteria. You can instruct the model to generate different content depending on the context or conditions.

Example: "If the user asks for a weather forecast, provide a summary of the day's weather. If they inquire about the weekend forecast, give a detailed outlook for both Saturday and Sunday."

Question-Answer Style Prompts: By structuring prompts in a question-and-answer format, you can generate content that directly addresses user queries. This technique is valuable for chatbots and customer support applications.

Example: "Question: What is the company's return policy? Answer: Our return policy allows for product returns within 30 days of purchase with a valid receipt."

Formatting and Stylistic Prompts: If you require content with a specific format or style, you can include formatting instructions in your prompts. This ensures that the AI generates content that adheres to your desired structure.

Example: "Generate a blog post in a 'listicle' format with five key tips for effective time management."

6.2 Enhancing Content Quality with Specialized Prompts

To enhance content quality, it's crucial to understand how to use specialized prompts effectively. Specialized prompts are tailored to different content types and objectives, ensuring that the AI generates content that aligns with your goals. Here are some examples:

Persuasive Prompts: When you need content to persuade or influence, use prompts that incorporate persuasive language and techniques.

Example: "Write a persuasive email to encourage subscribers to upgrade to the premium membership tier."

Comparative Prompts: To create content that compares different options or products, structure your prompts to guide the AI in presenting comparative information.

Example: "Compare the features and pricing of the three leading smartphones in the market and recommend the best choice for a budget-conscious consumer."

Descriptive Prompts: For content that describes a subject in detail, use descriptive prompts that guide the AI to provide comprehensive information.

Example: "Write a detailed travel guide for exploring the historic city of Rome, covering its iconic landmarks, culture, and local cuisine."

Educational Prompts: When the goal is to educate or inform, design prompts that encourage the AI to provide clear and informative explanations.

Example: "Create an informative infographic about the human digestive system, highlighting the key organs and their functions."

With the above examples, you would have now easily understood that your prompt should speak about the type and the degree of intensity of results that you are expecting from AI.

6.3 A/B Testing and Optimization

A/B testing is a powerful method for optimizing content generated by AI models. It involves creating multiple variations of content and testing them to determine which performs best. By analysing user interactions and feedback, you can refine your content strategy based on data-driven insights.

As usual let's go in simpler terms:

A/B Testing: Imagine you have a recipe for a cake, and you're not sure which icing is the tastiest— chocolate or vanilla. A/B testing is like having two cakes: one with chocolate icing (A) and one with vanilla icing (B). You share these cakes with friends and see which one they like more. Based on their feedback, you can decide which icing is better. It's a bit like a taste test to figure out what people prefer.

Optimization: Now, think of optimization as making the best cake possible. If you find out that most people like chocolate icing, you'll focus on making that cake even better. You might adjust the recipe to make it extra delicious. Optimization is like fine-tuning your cake recipe to make it as perfect as it can be. In the digital world, this means tweaking a website, app, or any other thing to make it work in the best possible way based on what people like. It's about making things better and better, just like perfecting a yummy cake recipe.

Example A/B Testing Scenario:

Objective: Optimize the product description for an e-commerce website to maximize conversions.

A/B Testing Variations:

Version A: The original product description generated by the AI.

Version B: A revised product description with more persuasive language and a stronger call to action.

Data-Driven Insights: After running both versions on the product page, analyze user interactions and conversion rates.

Results: If Version B leads to a higher conversion rate, you can conclude that the revised description is more effective and implement it on the website.

Case Studies on Maximizing Content Effectiveness

Let's explore real-world case studies that demonstrate how advanced prompt strategies and content optimization techniques have been applied to enhance content effectiveness.

Case Study 1: Email Marketing

Objective: Improve the click-through rate (CTR) of email marketing campaigns.

Advanced Strategies: The marketing team employed multi-step prompts to create email subject lines, body content, and calls to action. A/B testing was used to compare different email variations, measuring CTR and user engagement.

Results: By fine-tuning the prompts and optimizing content based on A/B testing insights, the CTR increased by 30%. The team discovered that subject lines with questions and personalized content were more effective in engaging recipients.

Case Study 2: Chatbot Conversations

Objective: Enhance the conversational experience of a customer support chatbot.

Advanced Strategies: The chatbot's prompts were structured in a question-answer format to address customer queries more directly. Conditional prompts were used to adapt responses based on customer needs.

Results: Customer satisfaction significantly improved, and the chatbot's accuracy in providing relevant information increased. The company reported a 25% reduction in support ticket volumes as a result of the chatbot's enhanced capabilities.

Case Study 3: Blog Content

Objective: Increase reader engagement and time spent on blog articles.

Advanced Strategies: For each blog post, specialized prompts were used to craft introductions, subheadings, and content in a format that encouraged easy reading. A/B testing was employed to assess variations in content structure and style.

Results: User engagement metrics showed a 40% increase in time spent on blog articles and a 15% rise in social media shares. The data revealed that articles with clear subheadings and concise paragraphs were preferred by readers.

Chapter 7: SEO and Content Optimization

In the digital age, effective online content is not just about creating engaging and informative material; it's also about ensuring that your content ranks well in search engine results. This chapter explores the relationship between SEO (Search Engine Optimization) and AI-generated content, providing insights on how to craft content for SEO success, the tools and strategies to optimize SEO, and how to measure the impact of SEO on AI-generated content.

Let's now put "Understanding SEO in AI-Generated Content" in simple terms:

Imagine you have a great story to tell, but you want lots of people to read it. SEO, or Search Engine Optimization, is like a magic spell that helps your story pop up when someone types keywords into a search engine, like Google. It's as if you're telling the search engine, "Hey, my story is about exciting adventures," and SEO makes sure your story shows up when someone searches for "exciting adventures."

Now, when it comes to AI-generated content, it's like you have a helpful robot who writes stories for you. SEO is a bit like teaching that robot to use the right words and phrases in your story so that search engines understand what it's about. This way, when people are looking for something similar to your story, the search engine knows to recommend it. SEO in AI-generated content is about making your robot writer speak the same language as the search engines, so your story gets the attention it deserves.

7.1 Understanding SEO in AI-Generated Content

What is SEO?

SEO, or Search Engine Optimization, is the practice of optimizing your online content so that it is more discoverable by search engines like Google, Bing, and Yahoo. When your content is optimized for SEO, it is more likely to appear at the top of search engine results pages (SERPs) when users search for relevant topics, keywords, or phrases.

The Importance of SEO

SEO is crucial for several reasons:

Increased Visibility: High-ranking content appears at the top of search results, making it more visible to users.

Traffic Generation: Content that ranks well attracts more organic traffic, reducing the need for paid advertising.

Credibility: High-ranking content is often perceived as more credible and trustworthy by users.

User Experience: SEO optimization improves the user experience by delivering relevant and high-quality content.

Competitive Advantage: Effective SEO can give you a competitive edge in the digital landscape.

AI-Generated Content and SEO

AI-generated content plays a significant role in SEO because it can be used to create vast amounts of content quickly, targeting specific keywords and topics. However, to be effective in SEO, AI-generated content needs to be crafted strategically.

7.2 Crafting Content for SEO Success

Keyword Research

Keyword research is the foundation of SEO content creation. It involves identifying the keywords and phrases that users are most likely to use when searching for content related to your topic or industry.

Let's make "keyword research" easy to understand:

Think of the internet like a massive library with billions of books. If you want to find a specific book in this library, you'd use keywords. Keywords are like magic words that help you discover the right books.

So, keyword research is the process of figuring out which magic words (keywords) people are using to search for things online. It's like becoming a detective to understand what words people type into search engines like Google when they're looking for information, products, or answers. Once you know these keywords, you can use them to make sure your website, blog, or content appears in the library when people are searching for the topics you're writing about. It's all about helping people find the right books (or web pages) in this vast online library.

Example: If you run a blog about travel, keywords like "best travel destinations 2023" or "budget travel tips" might be relevant.

pg. 91

High-Quality Content

While keywords are essential, high-quality content is equally crucial. Search engines reward content that is informative, engaging, and relevant to the user's search query.

Example: If your keyword is "healthy vegan recipes," your content should provide well-researched recipes, nutritional information, and cooking tips.

On-Page SEO

On-page SEO involves optimizing various elements within your content, including:

Title Tags: Crafting compelling and keyword-rich titles.

Meta Descriptions: Creating concise, informative meta descriptions.

Header Tags: Using header tags (H1, H2, H3, etc.) to structure your content.

Internal and External Links: Including relevant internal and external links.

Image Optimization: Adding alt text to images for accessibility and SEO.

Content-Length and Format

Long-form content tends to perform better in SEO, but it should still be well-structured and easy to read. Use bullet points, subheadings, and a logical flow to make your content more digestible.

Example: A 2,000-word article about "Digital Marketing Trends in 2023" is more likely to rank well compared to a 200-word article with the same topic.

7.3 Tools and Strategies for SEO Optimization

SEO Tools

Several tools can assist in SEO optimization:

Keyword Research Tools: Tools like Ahrefs, SEMrush, and Google's Keyword Planner help identify relevant keywords.

SEO Plugins: For content management systems like WordPress, plugins like Yoast SEO provide on-page SEO suggestions.

Analytics Tools: Google Analytics and Google Search Console offer insights into website performance and user behaviour.

Content Analysis Tools: Tools like Grammarly and Hemingway Editor can help improve content quality.

Link Building

Building a network of high-quality backlinks to your content from authoritative websites can significantly improve your SEO ranking.

Example: If a reputable technology website links to your blog post about the latest tech trends, it enhances the credibility and authority of your content in the eyes of search engines.

Mobile Optimization

With a growing number of users accessing content on mobile devices, ensuring that your content is mobile-friendly is essential for SEO.

Example: Mobile optimization includes responsive design, fast loading times, and legible text on smaller screens.

Local SEO

For businesses with a physical presence, local SEO is vital. It involves optimizing content for local search, including location-specific keywords and information.

Example: If you run a bakery, optimizing for "best bakery in [Your City]" can attract local customers.

7.4 Measuring SEO Impact on AI-Generated Content

Measuring the impact of SEO on AI-generated content is crucial for ongoing improvement. Here are key metrics and methods for evaluation:

Keyword Rankings

Track how your content is ranking for targeted keywords. Tools like Google Search Console and rank tracking software provide insights into keyword performance.

Example: If your content ranks on the first page for a competitive keyword, it indicates successful SEO optimization.

Organic Traffic

Monitor the organic traffic to your AI-generated content. An increase in organic traffic demonstrates that your content is resonating with users and search engines.

Example: If the number of visitors to your blog post about "Digital Marketing Strategies" doubles after SEO optimization, it's a positive sign.

Click-Through Rate (CTR)

The CTR indicates the percentage of users who click on your content in search results. Higher CTR suggests that your content is appealing to users.

Example: If your CTR for a blog post about "Healthy Meal Plans" increases from 3% to 10% after SEO optimization, it's a significant improvement.

Bounce Rate

The bounce rate measures the percentage of users who leave your website without interacting further. A lower bounce rate indicates that users find your content engaging.

Example: If your bounce rate for a landing page about "Eco-Friendly Products" decreases from 70% to 30% after SEO optimization, it's a positive change.

Conversion Rate

For businesses, the conversion rate is a crucial metric. It measures how many users take a desired action, such as making a purchase or filling out a contact form.

Example: If your e-commerce product page for "Organic Skincare Products" sees a 20% increase in conversions after SEO optimization, it demonstrates the positive impact on business goals.

Chapter 8: Content Generation for Websites

8.1 Methods of creating Content

There are several methods for content generation for websites, each tailored to different needs and goals. Here are some common methods:

Original Content: Creating unique and original content from scratch is a fundamental approach. This can include articles, blog posts, product descriptions, and more. It's ideal for establishing your brand's voice and authority.

Curated Content: Curating content involves gathering and sharing relevant articles, images, or videos from other sources on your website. It's a good way to provide valuable resources to your audience and build credibility.

User-Generated Content (UGC): Encouraging users to contribute content, such as reviews, comments, or guest posts, can help foster community engagement and enhance your website's value.

Content Repurposing: Take existing content and repurpose it into different formats. For example, you can turn a blog post into a video, an infographic, or a podcast episode to reach a wider audience.

Content Aggregators: Use automation tools or plugins to aggregate content from various sources and display it on your website. This can be useful for news websites or niche-specific content hubs.

Collaborative Content: Collaborate with other content creators, experts, or influencers in your niche to co-author content or conduct interviews. This can help expand your reach and authority.

Video Content: Creating video content, such as tutorials, interviews, or product demonstrations, is a popular method to engage audiences, especially on platforms like YouTube.

Visual Content: Visual elements like infographics, images, and slideshows can convey information in a visually appealing manner and complement text-based content.

Podcasts: Podcasts have gained popularity as a content format. They allow you to share information, conduct interviews, and build a loyal following.

AI-Generated Content: AI-powered tools and models can assist in generating content. For instance, they can create product descriptions, generate reports, or even write articles. However, this should be done with caution to ensure quality and authenticity.

The choice of content generation method depends on your website's purpose, your target audience, and your available resources. Often, a mix of these methods can provide a well-rounded and engaging user experience on your website.

In today's digital age, websites serve as the online face of businesses and individuals, making the quality and relevance of content paramount. AI-driven content generation has become a valuable asset in populating websites with engaging, informative, and consistent material. This chapter delves into the various aspects of using AI to create website content, the roles it plays in blog posts and articles, provides examples of AI-generated website content, and offers guidance on maintaining consistency in voice and style.

8.2 Using AI to Create Website Content

The Transformative Power of AI

Artificial Intelligence has revolutionized content generation for websites. AI-driven tools and models can swiftly produce vast amounts of text, adhere to specific style guidelines, and even optimize content for search engines (SEO). This enables website owners to keep their pages fresh, informative, and appealing to visitors.

Types of Website Content Generated by AI

Product Descriptions: AI can create detailed and persuasive product descriptions for e-commerce websites, helping potential buyers make informed decisions.

Blog Posts: AI can generate blog posts on a wide range of topics, including news, how-to guides, and opinion pieces.

News Updates: For news websites, AI can produce timely and accurate news articles based on data and events.

FAQs and Knowledge Bases: AI can create comprehensive FAQs and knowledge bases for customer support and information sharing.

Service Descriptions: AI can draft service descriptions that convey the value and benefits of services offered by businesses.

8.3 The Role of AI in Blog Posts and Articles

Faster Content Generation

Blog posts and articles are crucial for websites to engage with readers and provide value. AI can expedite the content generation process, allowing websites to publish more frequently.

Example: A news website can use AI to create breaking news articles within minutes of an event, keeping readers informed in real-time.

Content Personalization

AI-driven content can be tailored to suit the interests and preferences of individual readers. This personalization increases reader engagement and retention.

Example: An online magazine can use AI to recommend and generate articles based on a user's past reading history and interests.

Data-Driven Insights

AI can analyse data and generate insightful articles based on trends, statistics, and research, making data-driven journalism more accessible.

Example: A financial news website can use AI to analyse stock market data and generate reports on market trends and investment opportunities.

Multilingual Capabilities

AI can quickly translate content into multiple languages, enabling websites to reach a global audience.

Example: An e-commerce website can use AI to translate product descriptions into various languages, broadening its customer base.

Examples of AI-Generated Website Content

E-commerce Product Descriptions

AI can create compelling and informative product descriptions, helping customers make purchasing decisions.

Example: An online fashion retailer can use AI to generate product descriptions that highlight the fabric, design, and unique selling points of each clothing item.

News Articles

For news websites, AI can generate breaking news articles that provide concise information about current events.

Example: A news website can use AI to quickly draft articles about natural disasters, including details like location, severity, and safety measures.

How-To Guides

AI-generated how-to guides are useful for websites offering tutorials and educational content.

Example: A cooking website can use AI to generate step-by-step guides on preparing popular recipes, complete with ingredient lists and cooking tips.

Blog Posts

AI can create blog posts on a variety of topics, from technology and health to travel and lifestyle.

Example: A travel blog can use AI to draft articles about destination highlights, travel tips, and cultural experiences.

Service Descriptions

AI-generated service descriptions can effectively communicate the value of a business's offerings.

Example: A digital marketing agency's website can use AI to create service descriptions that emphasize the benefits of their SEO and content marketing services.

Ensuring Consistency in Voice and Style

Consistency in voice and style is essential for maintaining the reputation and branding of a website. Here's how to achieve this while using AI for content generation:

Style Guidelines: Develop clear style guidelines that detail the tone, voice, and style of content. Ensure that AI models are programmed to adhere to these guidelines.

Training AI: Train AI models on a specific writing style by providing them with examples of the desired style and tone.

Editing and Review: Assign human editors to review AI-generated content for consistency and quality. They can make necessary adjustments to align the content with the website's style guidelines.

Feedback Loop: Establish a feedback loop where editors provide AI with feedback on its content to improve its performance over time.

Customization: Fine-tune AI models to suit your website's unique voice and style. This can involve adjusting the models' parameters and training them specifically for your website.

Consistency Checks: Regularly monitor content for consistency, both within individual pieces and across the entire website. This can ensure that your website has consistency in maintaining the originality, and regularity in updating the information.

Chapter 9: Social Media and AI Content

Social media is a dynamic and ever-evolving platform for communication and engagement. The integration of AI in social media content creation has revolutionized the way businesses and individuals interact with their audience. In this chapter, we explore how AI is used to create engaging social media posts, personalize content for different platforms, and provide case studies of AI-generated social media content. We also delve into the ethical considerations surrounding AI-powered social media marketing.

Social Media: Think of social media like a giant bulletin board where people share their thoughts, photos, and updates. It's like having conversations with friends, but instead of talking in person, you're doing it online. You can post about your day, share interesting things you find, or chat with others. Social media platforms, such as Facebook, Instagram, and Twitter, are like different types of bulletin boards where you can join in and connect with people from all over.

AI Content: Now, AI content is like having a super-smart assistant. It can help you write posts, generate ideas, or even create cool images and videos for your social media. It's like having a creative friend who's really good with words and pictures. AI can make your social media posts more interesting and save you time. It's as if you have a digital helper making your bulletin board look amazing and engaging for everyone who stops by. So, social media and AI content go hand in hand, making your online conversations more exciting and enjoyable.

9.1 Creating Engaging Social Media Posts with AI

The Power of Engagement

Engagement is at the core of social media success. Engaging social media posts not only capture the audience's attention but also encourage interactions such as likes, shares, comments, and click-throughs.

AI in Content Creation

AI has brought a new level of efficiency and creativity to content creation for social media. Here's how AI contributes to creating engaging social media posts:

Content Generation: AI can generate text, images, and videos that are optimized for various social media platforms.

Personalization: AI can tailor content to specific audiences, taking into account user preferences and behaviours.

Trend Analysis: AI can analyse trends and real-time data to ensure that content is relevant and timely.

A/B Testing: AI can help identify the most effective content variations through A/B testing, maximizing engagement.

Example: An e-commerce brand can use AI to create engaging social media posts that feature product images, compelling copy, and personalized product recommendations based on a user's browsing history.

9.2 Personalizing Content for Different Platforms

Platform Diversity

Different social media platforms have unique characteristics and user expectations. Successful social media marketing involves adapting content to fit the platform.

AI-Powered Personalization

AI allows for the personalization of content based on platform-specific guidelines. Here's how AI can personalize content for different platforms:

Adapting Content Length: AI can adjust the length of posts to match the platform's character limits. For instance, shorter text for Twitter and longer descriptions for Instagram.

Content Format: AI can generate images, videos, carousels, and stories optimized for each platform.

Audience Segmentation: AI can categorize and target content based on audience demographics, interests, and behaviour on each platform.

Example: A media company can use AI to create engaging short video clips for platforms like TikTok, while crafting long-form articles for LinkedIn to cater to different audience expectations.

9.3 Case Studies of AI-Generated Social Media Content

Let's explore case studies that exemplify the successful use of AI in social media content creation.

Case Study 1: Personalized Product Recommendations

Objective: An e-commerce company sought to boost its social media engagement and conversion rates.

AI Solution: The company employed AI to analyse user browsing and purchase history. It generated personalized product recommendations for each user.

Results: Social media posts featuring personalized product recommendations led to a 20% increase in click-through rates and a 15% increase in conversions. Users appreciated the tailored content and the convenience of discovering products they were interested in.

Case Study 2: Real-Time Trend Analysis

Objective: A fashion brand aimed to stay ahead of fashion trends and engage with a younger audience on social media.

AI Solution: The brand used AI to analyse real-time fashion trends and generated posts that highlighted trending styles.

Results: The brand's social media engagement increased by 30%, and they gained a significant following among trend-conscious consumers. AI's ability to identify emerging trends allowed the brand to maintain a fresh and relevant presence.

Case Study 3: Platform-Specific Content

Objective: A travel agency wanted to expand its social media reach and connect with travellers on different platforms.

AI Solution: AI was employed to tailor content for specific platforms. It generated vibrant images for Instagram, travel guides for Pinterest, and interactive quizzes for Facebook.

Results: The agency experienced a 40% increase in social media followers, and users praised the diversity of content tailored to each platform. AI's adaptability allowed the agency to engage with a wider audience.

9.4 Ethics in AI-Powered Social Media Marketing

Ethical considerations are critical when using AI in social media marketing. Here are key ethical aspects to be mindful of:

Transparency: Inform your audience when content is generated by AI to maintain trust and transparency.

Privacy: Safeguard user data and comply with privacy regulations. AI should respect user privacy and not infringe on data rights.

Bias and Fairness: Ensure that AI-generated content is free from bias and discrimination, promoting fairness and inclusivity.

User Consent: Respect user consent for data collection and ensure that users have control over their data.

Review and Accountability: Regularly review AI-generated content for compliance with ethical guidelines and establish accountability for any breaches.

Balancing Automation and Human Oversight: Strive for a balance between automation and human review to maintain quality and ethical standards.

Example: A fashion brand using AI for personalized fashion recommendations should clearly state when recommendations are AI-generated, obtain user consent for data use, and regularly review AI recommendations to avoid promoting biased or discriminatory content.

Chapter 10: Email Marketing and Newsletters

Email marketing remains a cornerstone of digital communication and outreach. The integration of Artificial Intelligence (AI) has brought significant enhancements to email marketing, from crafting compelling email copy to boosting subscriber engagement through AI-generated newsletters. This chapter explores the power of AI in email marketing, provides insights on creating persuasive email copy, offers strategies to enhance subscriber engagement through AI-generated newsletters, and delves into the analysis of AI's impact on email marketing.

To put it in simple terms, Email marketing is like sending letters to your friends, but it's done through the internet. Instead of using a pen and paper, you use your computer to write a message and send it to a bunch of people all at once. These messages can be about all sorts of things – like sharing news, telling stories, or even letting people know about cool stuff you have for sale. It's like having your own newsletter that you can send to people who want to hear from you.

Here's the clever part: with email marketing, you can keep track of who opens your letters and what they're interested in. It's a bit like knowing which parts of your stories your friends like the most. So, you can send them more of what they enjoy. Email marketing helps you stay in touch with your friends and share things you think they'll love, all while knowing what makes them smile!

10.1 The Power of AI in Email Marketing

Relevance and Personalization

Email marketing's effectiveness lies in delivering relevant and personalized content to subscribers. AI plays a pivotal role in achieving this level of precision.

Key AI Features for Email Marketing:

Personalization: AI can analyse subscriber behaviour and preferences to deliver tailored content.

Segmentation: AI can segment subscribers based on demographics, behaviour, and preferences.

Recommendations: AI can generate product or content recommendations specific to each subscriber.

A/B Testing: AI can run A/B tests to determine the most effective subject lines, content, and send times.

Example: An online bookstore can use AI to analyze a customer's past purchases and generate personalized book recommendations in their email newsletters.

10.2 Crafting Compelling Email Copy with AI

Subject Lines

The subject line is the gateway to your email. AI can optimize subject lines for open rates by considering factors like relevance, personalization, and urgency.

Example: AI can analyse user behaviour and craft subject lines like "Discover Your Next Adventure - Recommended Just for You."

Content Generation

AI can generate engaging email content, including articles, product descriptions, event promotions, and more.

Example: An e-commerce company can use AI to create product descriptions, emphasizing unique features and benefits.

Call-to-Action (CTA)

AI can suggest compelling CTAs that encourage readers to take the desired action.

Example: AI can generate CTAs like "Shop Now," "Learn More," or "Start Your Free Trial," which are known to drive clicks.

Personalization

AI can customize email content based on subscriber data, such as name, location, and browsing history.

Example: An online fashion retailer can use AI to personalize emails with the subscriber's name and offer clothing recommendations based on past purchases.

Dynamic Content

AI can create dynamic content that changes based on subscriber actions and preferences.

Example: An airline can use AI to send emails with dynamically generated flight offers that change based on the subscriber's destination preferences.

10.3 Subscriber Engagement through AI-Generated Newsletters

Content Recommendations

AI-powered newsletters provide personalized content recommendations to subscribers.

Example: A technology news website can use AI to send weekly newsletters with personalized article recommendations based on the subscriber's interests.

Behavioural Targeting

AI can analyse subscriber behaviour to send targeted newsletters, promoting relevant products or content.

Example: An online magazine can send a newsletter featuring articles on topics the subscriber has recently shown interest in.

Drip Campaigns

AI can automate drip email campaigns that send a series of emails to nurture leads and guide subscribers through the customer journey.

Example: A software company can use AI to set up a drip campaign that educates potential customers about their product features and benefits.

Personalized Offers

AI can create emails with tailored offers and discounts to encourage conversions.

Example: An e-commerce brand can use AI to send subscribers exclusive discounts on products they've shown interest in.

Event Announcements

AI can send event announcements and reminders to subscribers.

Example: An event management company can use AI to send emails with event details, registration links, and personalized reminders.

10.4 Analysing the Impact of AI on Email Marketing

To measure the impact of AI on email marketing, businesses should consider key performance metrics and conduct thorough analyses.

Open Rates

AI-optimized subject lines and personalized content often lead to higher open rates.

Example: An AI-driven email campaign for a fashion brand resulted in a 20% increase in open rates compared to previous non-AI campaigns.

Click-Through Rates (CTR)

AI-generated content and recommendations can significantly improve CTR.

Example: A retail company saw a 30% increase in CTR after implementing AI to personalize product recommendations in email newsletters.

Conversion Rates

AI can drive higher conversion rates by delivering personalized offers and content.

Example: A software company witnessed a 25% increase in conversion rates in a drip campaign using AI-generated content and personalized recommendations.

Subscriber Retention

AI-generated content that is engaging and personalized can contribute to improved subscriber retention rates.

Example: A subscription-based streaming service experienced a 15% reduction in subscriber churn after implementing AI to deliver personalized content recommendations in their email newsletters.

Revenue

Higher engagement, CTR, and conversion rates ultimately lead to increased revenue.

Example: A travel booking platform reported a 40% boost in revenue attributed to AI-driven email campaigns that recommended personalized travel packages.

AI's integration into email marketing has revolutionized the way businesses engage with subscribers. The power of AI is evident in its ability to craft compelling email copy, personalize content, enhance subscriber engagement through AI-generated newsletters, and drive improved performance metrics. Analysing the impact of AI on email marketing reveals higher open rates, CTR, conversion rates, subscriber retention, and revenue, demonstrating that AI is a valuable asset for businesses looking to connect with their audience through email.

Chapter 11: Chatbots and Virtual Assistants

In the world of customer service and digital interaction, chatbots and virtual assistants have become invaluable tools. The integration of Artificial Intelligence (AI) has significantly enhanced their capabilities, making interactions more efficient, personalized, and human-like. This chapter explores how AI enhances chatbot and virtual assistant conversations, the importance of effective prompts in building conversational AI, real-world examples of AI-powered chatbots, and user experience considerations in the use of AI in chatbot and virtual assistant interactions.

Let's make "chatbots and virtual assistants" simple to understand.

Chatbots: Chatbots are like friendly robots that you can chat with, just like texting a friend. They live inside your computer or phone and can help you with all sorts of things. For example, if you have a question about the weather, you can type it, and the chatbot will give you the answer. It's a bit like having a smart buddy who's always ready to chat and provide information or help you with tasks.

Virtual Assistants: Virtual assistants are like your personal helpers, but they live in your device, too. You can talk to them, and they can do things for you. For instance, you can say, "Set an alarm for 7 AM," and your virtual assistant will make sure you wake up on time. It's like having a digital friend who's super organized and can take care of tasks like sending messages, setting reminders, or even answering questions. Both chatbots and virtual assistants are like having helpful companions right in your phone or computer, ready to assist you.

11.1 How AI Enhances Chatbot and Virtual Assistant Conversations

Natural Language Processing

AI brings the power of natural language processing (NLP) to chatbots and virtual assistants. NLP enables these digital entities to understand and respond to human language in a more human-like manner.

Key AI Features in Conversations:

Understanding Context: AI can track and interpret the context of a conversation, allowing for more coherent and relevant responses.

Personalization: AI can analyse user data and tailor responses based on user preferences and history.

Multilingual Support: AI can converse with users in multiple languages, broadening the accessibility of chatbots and virtual assistants.

Emotion Detection: Advanced AI can identify user emotions and adapt responses accordingly.

Example: A virtual assistant can use AI to understand and respond appropriately to a user's request for restaurant recommendations, considering the user's previous dining preferences and current location.

11.2 Building Conversational AI with Effective Prompts

Prompts and Training

Effective prompts are essential in training AI for chatbots and virtual assistants. Prompts serve as the foundation for building AI models that understand and respond to user queries.

Components of Effective Prompts:

Clarity: Prompts should be clear and well-structured, ensuring the AI understands the desired context and intent.

Variety: A range of prompts helps train AI to handle different user inputs effectively.

Real Data: Prompts should be based on real user interactions and queries to align AI with real-world scenarios.

Ethical Considerations: Prompts should be designed with ethical considerations to avoid generating harmful or inappropriate responses.

Example: To train a virtual assistant for a healthcare chatbot, prompts may include questions about symptoms, medication, and medical history, ensuring that the AI is well-prepared to assist users with health-related queries.

11.3 Real-World Examples of AI-Powered Chatbots

Customer Support

Many businesses employ AI-powered chatbots for customer support. These chatbots can answer common questions, troubleshoot issues, and escalate complex problems to human agents.

Example: An e-commerce platform uses a chatbot that employs AI to assist customers with order tracking, refunds, and product inquiries. The chatbot can also offer personalized product recommendations based on user browsing history.

Virtual Shopping Assistants

Virtual shopping assistants utilize AI to help users find products, provide information, and offer purchase recommendations.

Example: A clothing retailer's virtual assistant can use AI to ask users about their style preferences, budget, and occasion, and then suggest suitable clothing items.

Language Learning

AI-powered chatbots have been used to assist individuals in learning new languages, providing conversational practice and feedback.

Example: A language learning app uses an AI-powered chatbot to engage users in dialogues, correct pronunciation, and offer vocabulary exercises in the user's target language.

Personal Finance

Chatbots can assist with personal finance, offering budgeting advice, tracking expenses, and providing financial insights.

Example: A personal finance chatbot uses AI to categorize and analyse a user's spending patterns, offering personalized budgeting recommendations and investment strategies.

11.4 User Experience Considerations

Seamlessness

For a positive user experience, chatbot interactions should feel seamless and human-like. This involves a few key considerations:

Response Time: Fast and accurate responses ensure users don't experience delays or frustration.

Tone and Language: AI responses should be friendly, respectful, and in a language that the user is comfortable with.

Escalation: There should be a clear path for users to escalate to human agents when AI cannot fulfil their needs.

Example: A virtual assistant for a travel website should offer prompt and courteous responses, be adept at helping users find and book flights and hotels, and provide a smooth transition to a human agent if necessary.

Data Privacy

User data privacy is a paramount concern in chatbot and virtual assistant interactions. It is crucial to protect user information and comply with data protection regulations.

Example: A financial chatbot should assure users that their banking information and financial details are stored securely and that the chatbot adheres to banking industry data protection standards.

Feedback and Improvement

Feedback mechanisms should be in place to allow users to provide input and help improve the chatbot's performance over time.

Example: An AI chatbot used for restaurant reservations should encourage users to rate their experience and provide comments, allowing the system to improve reservation recommendations and customer service.

AI has brought transformative capabilities to chatbots and virtual assistants, making them more responsive, personalized, and user-friendly. The development of effective prompts is key to training

AI, ensuring that it understands and responds to user queries effectively. Real-world examples showcase the diverse applications of AI-powered chatbots in customer support, virtual shopping, language learning, and personal finance. User experience considerations, including seamlessness, data privacy, and feedback mechanisms, are essential to ensure that AI-powered chatbot interactions are user-centric and valuable.

Chapter 12: E-commerce and Product Descriptions

E-commerce has revolutionized the way we shop, and one of its critical components is the product description. In recent years, Artificial Intelligence (AI) has played a significant role in optimizing product descriptions, making them more appealing, informative, and engaging. This chapter explores how AI enhances e-commerce product descriptions, showcases examples of AI-generated product descriptions, and emphasizes the importance of monitoring customer response and conversion rates for e-commerce success.

Let's simplify things to understand easily the terms "e-commerce and product description."

E-commerce: E-commerce is like having a shopping mall on the internet. Instead of going to a physical store, you can visit websites on your computer or phone to buy things. You can browse through different sections, like clothing or electronics, and choose what you want. It's a bit like having the entire mall at your fingertips, and you can shop anytime, anywhere.

Product Description: When you're shopping online, you want to know all about the things you're buying, right? That's where product descriptions come in. They're like little information cards that tell you everything about the product – what it looks like, how it works, and why it's awesome. It's like having a friend explain why a new gadget or a dress is so great. Product descriptions help you make smart choices when you're shopping in the online mall.

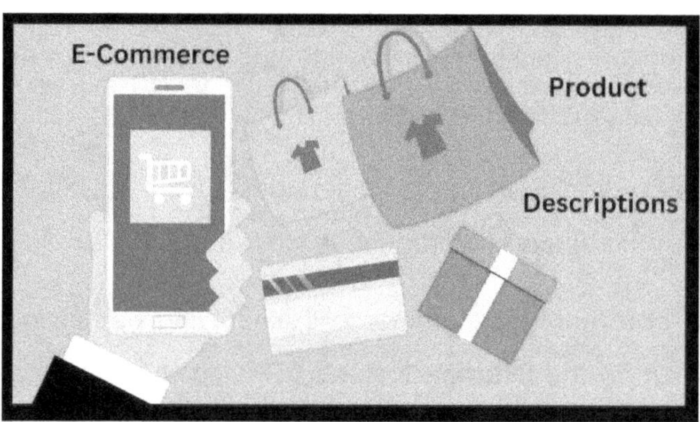

pg. 134

12.1 Optimizing Product Descriptions with AI

The Significance of Product Descriptions

In the world of e-commerce, product descriptions are the bridge between the consumer and the product. They must be accurate, persuasive, and informative to drive purchasing decisions.

AI-Powered Enhancements

AI brings several enhancements to product descriptions:

Personalization: AI can tailor product descriptions based on user preferences and behaviour.

Optimization: AI can optimize descriptions for search engines, enhancing product visibility.

Multilingual Capabilities: AI can quickly translate descriptions, broadening the potential customer base.

Data Analysis: AI can analyse customer data to identify the most effective descriptors and selling points.

Example: An online electronics store uses AI to personalize product descriptions for users who have a history of purchasing high-end gadgets. The descriptions highlight advanced features, quality, and performance to cater to these customers' preferences.

12.2 AI-Generated Descriptions for E-commerce

Automating Content Creation

AI can generate product descriptions at scale, saving time and resources. These descriptions can be tailored to specific products, ensuring relevance and accuracy.

Key Elements in AI-Generated Descriptions:

Product Features: AI can extract and highlight essential features, such as dimensions, materials, and specifications.

Benefits and Use Cases: AI can provide information about how the product can benefit the user and its potential applications.

Emotion and Persuasion: AI can incorporate persuasive language to encourage purchases, such as mentioning limited stock or discounts.

Search Engine Optimization (SEO): AI can optimize descriptions with keywords to improve search engine rankings.

Example: An AI-generated description for a digital camera may highlight features like high-resolution sensors, zoom capabilities, and low-light performance. It would emphasize the camera's ability to capture precious memories and suggest its suitability for photography enthusiasts.

12.3 Examples of AI-Enhanced Product Descriptions

Let's explore real-world examples of AI-enhanced product descriptions in various e-commerce sectors:

Fashion and Apparel

In the fashion industry, AI can generate dynamic product descriptions that change based on user preferences. For instance, a description for a dress can emphasize different aspects like style, material, or colour based on the user's preferences.

Example: An AI-generated product description for a dress may highlight its breathable fabric, versatile style, or vibrant colour based on the user's previous choices or browsing history.

Electronics and Gadgets

For electronic products, AI can provide detailed specifications and benefits, ensuring that users have all the necessary information to make informed choices.

Example: An AI-generated description for a smartphone can include technical specifications like processor speed, camera resolution, and battery life, along with benefits like fast performance and stunning photography capabilities.

Home and Furniture

In the home and furniture category, AI can create product descriptions that consider aspects like size, materials, design, and suitability for different room settings.

Example: An AI-generated description for a sofa can emphasize its size, upholstery material, modern design, and its versatility in fitting various room aesthetics.

Food and Beverages

Even in the food and beverage industry, AI can be used to create enticing product descriptions. These descriptions may focus on taste, ingredients, nutritional value, and serving suggestions.

Example: An AI-generated description for a gourmet coffee blend can highlight its rich flavour profile, the blend of premium beans, its caffeine content, and suggestions for brewing the perfect cup.

12.4 Monitoring Customer Response and Conversion Rates

The Importance of Feedback

In the e-commerce world, product descriptions should be continuously refined based on customer response and conversion rates. AI can help in this by monitoring and analysing user interactions and preferences.

Key Metrics to Monitor:

Conversion Rate: The percentage of users who make a purchase after viewing the product description.

Click-Through Rate (CTR): The ratio of users who click on the product description to the total number of users who viewed it.

Time Spent on Page: The duration users spend reading the product description.

User Feedback: Comments, reviews, and ratings provided by users regarding the product and description quality.

Purchase History: Analysing which descriptions led to higher sales can help refine future descriptions.

Example: An e-commerce platform may notice that product descriptions with a focus on specific features and benefits receive higher conversion rates. They can use this data to tailor descriptions for other similar products.

AI has ushered in a new era of e-commerce product descriptions. It offers personalization, optimization, multilingual capabilities, and data-driven enhancements to create engaging and persuasive descriptions. Real-world examples from fashion, electronics, home, and food sectors highlight the versatility of AI in enhancing product descriptions. Monitoring customer response and conversion rates is crucial to refining descriptions and driving sales in the competitive e-commerce landscape. As e-commerce continues to evolve, AI will remain a pivotal tool for delivering product information that is not only informative but also compelling.

Chapter 13: Legal and Ethical Considerations

In the era of Artificial Intelligence (AI), the generation of content through machine learning models has brought about numerous legal and ethical concerns. This chapter delves into the legal aspects of AI-generated content, ensuring compliance with copyright and plagiarism laws, addressing ethical considerations in AI content generation, and emphasizing the importance of user consent and transparency in this ever-evolving landscape.

Imagine AI-generated content is like having a robot that helps you write things. Now, like all things, there are rules for what the robot can and can't do. That's where the legal aspects come in. It's like the robot having a set of guidelines to follow, just like you have rules to follow at home or at school.

These guidelines are there to make sure the content the robot creates is fair, safe, and doesn't break any laws. It's a bit like how you have to follow the road rules when you ride your bike to make sure you're safe and not causing any problems. So, the legal aspects of AI-generated content are about making sure everything the robot writes is done in the right way, following the rules, and not causing any trouble.

13.1 Legal Aspects of AI-Generated Content

Intellectual Property Rights

AI-generated content can potentially infringe on intellectual property rights, particularly copyrights, trademarks, and patents. It's essential to understand how these laws apply to AI-generated content.

Key Legal Considerations:

Copyright Ownership: In many jurisdictions, the creator of a work, whether human or AI, is granted copyright ownership. Determining authorship in AI-generated content can be legally complex.

Fair Use: The concept of fair use allows limited use of copyrighted material without permission from the copyright holder. It's essential to ascertain whether AI-generated content complies with fair use principles.

Public Domain: Content generated by AI may fall into the public domain, making it exempt from copyright restrictions. However, this depends on local copyright laws and regulations.

Derivative Works: AI-generated content that is derived from copyrighted material may require permission from the original content creator.

Example: An AI-generated artwork heavily inspired by a famous painting could potentially infringe on the original artist's copyright. Determining the legality of this AI-generated piece involves examining the jurisdiction's copyright laws.

13.2 Ensuring Compliance with Copyright and Plagiarism Laws

Copyright Infringement

AI-generated content should be thoroughly reviewed to ensure it does not infringe upon the copyrights of other works. This is particularly important in fields such as journalism, literature, and art.

Preventing Copyright Infringement:

Originality: AI models should be trained on original and legally obtained data.

Attribution: Properly attribute sources if AI-generated content incorporates elements from other works.

Permission: Seek permission from copyright holders when creating derivative AI content based on their copyrighted works.

Public Domain: Be aware of works in the public domain and follow the respective usage guidelines.

Example: An AI-generated article for a news website must ensure that the content is original and does not infringe upon the copyright of other news sources, even if it covers the same topic.

Plagiarism

AI-generated content can also be susceptible to plagiarism if it replicates or closely resembles existing works. Avoiding plagiarism is crucial for maintaining ethical content generation.

Preventing Plagiarism:

pg. 145

Citations: Use citations and references where appropriate to give credit to the original creators of concepts and ideas.

Paraphrasing: Encourage AI models to paraphrase and restructure existing content rather than directly copying it.

Original Data: Train AI models on original data and ensure they do not rely solely on existing, copyrighted content.

Example: An AI-generated academic paper should provide citations for studies and research it refers to, acknowledging the original authors and sources.

13.3. Ethical Use of AI in Content Generation

Bias and Discrimination

AI models can inadvertently perpetuate bias and discrimination found in training data. It is essential to address this ethical issue.

Avoiding Bias and Discrimination:

Diverse Training Data: Train AI models on diverse datasets to reduce bias.

Bias Evaluation: Regularly evaluate AI-generated content for bias, especially when it concerns sensitive topics or demographics.

Ethical Guidelines: Establish ethical guidelines for AI content generation that prioritize fairness and inclusivity.

Example: An AI model generating job advertisements should be programmed to avoid biased language that may discriminate against certain groups.

Privacy

Respecting user privacy is a fundamental ethical consideration in AI-generated content, particularly when collecting and using personal data.

Privacy Best Practices:

Consent: Always obtain user consent for data collection and usage.

Data Protection: Ensure that user data is stored securely and protected from unauthorized access.

Transparency: Clearly communicate to users how their data will be used and for what purposes.

Example: An AI chatbot should inform users that their conversations may be recorded for quality assurance but should not be used for other purposes without explicit consent.

13.4 User Consent and Transparency

Informed Consent

User consent is a cornerstone of ethical AI content generation. Users should be fully informed about how their data and interactions with AI-generated content will be used.

Ensuring Informed Consent:

Clear Information: Provide clear and easily accessible information about data usage and AI-generated content.

Opt-In and Opt-Out: Give users the choice to opt in or opt out of data collection and AI content generation.

Revocable Consent: Allow users to revoke their consent at any time and have their data deleted.

Example: An AI-powered personal assistant should inform users during setup about data collection and processing for personalized services and seek their explicit consent before proceeding.

Transparency

Transparency is essential to build trust with users. They should be aware that they are interacting with AI-generated content and not human-generated content.

Ensuring Transparency:

Disclosure: Clearly disclose when content is AI-generated, such as marking chatbot interactions or news articles as "AI-generated."

User Awareness: Educate users about the capabilities and limitations of AI-generated content.

Ethical Guidelines: Implement guidelines to ensure transparency in AI-generated content creation.

Example: A news website using AI to generate news articles should add a disclaimer at the beginning of each AI-generated article, informing readers that it was generated by an AI model.

Legal and ethical considerations in AI-generated content are paramount in a world where technology increasingly influences content creation. Understanding the legal aspects related to copyright and plagiarism is crucial to avoid legal disputes. Ethical considerations involve addressing bias, discrimination, and respecting user privacy. Ensuring user consent and transparency builds trust and ensures that users are aware of their interactions with AI-generated content. As AI continues to play a significant role in content generation, adherence to these principles will be central to ethical and legally compliant content creation in various domains.

Chapter 14: Future Trends in AI-Generated Content

As technology advances at a rapid pace, the field of AI-generated content continues to evolve. This chapter explores the future trends and emerging technologies in AI content generation, providing examples and insights into how these developments are shaping various industries and content creation processes.

14.1 Future Trends

1. Generative Adversarial Networks (GANs)

What Are GANs?

Generative Adversarial Networks, or GANs, are a class of machine learning models that involve two neural networks, a generator, and a discriminator, working in a competitive manner. The generator creates content, and the discriminator evaluates it. Over time, this dynamic leads to the creation of high-quality, realistic content.

Generative Adversarial Networks, or GANs for short, are like a pair of artists working together to create something amazing. Imagine one artist is a forger, and the other is an art detective.

The forger's job is to make fake paintings that look like famous artworks. These are the "generated" artworks. The art detective's job is to figure out which paintings are fake and which are real. They "adversarily" challenge each other.

As they play this artistic game, the forger gets better and better at making realistic fakes, and the detective gets sharper at spotting them. This competition pushes them both to improve, and in the end, you get really convincing fake art. GANs are used in computers to generate things like realistic images, videos, or even music by pitting two computer programs against each other, like the forger and the detective. It's like a creative duel that results in impressive computer-generated content.

Application Examples:

Art and Design: GANs have been used to generate art, create new designs, and even produce realistic-looking human faces for various industries, from video games to marketing.

Content Automation: In content creation, GANs can be employed to generate image descriptions, create realistic product images, or even generate marketing materials.

Challenges: Ethical concerns surrounding deepfake technology and the misuse of GANs for misleading content are challenges to be addressed.

2. Multimodal AI Content Generation

Combining Text and Images

Multimodal AI content generation is about combining text and images to create content. This approach opens up exciting possibilities in various industries, including marketing, advertising, and entertainment.

Application Examples:

Interactive Content: Imagine reading a book where the illustrations are generated based on your descriptions of the scenes, providing a unique reading experience for every reader.

Product Descriptions: In e-commerce, combining textual product descriptions with AI-generated images can create immersive and informative product listings.

pg. 153

Challenges: Ensuring that the combination of text and images results in coherent and meaningful content is a challenge that requires fine-tuning.

3. Conversational AI

AI-Powered Conversations

Conversational AI, often driven by powerful language models like GPT-4, is reshaping customer support, chatbots, and virtual assistants.

Application Examples:

Customer Support: AI-driven chatbots can engage in more natural, context-aware conversations, providing better support and reducing response times.

Content Creation: Conversational AI can assist content creators by generating ideas, summaries, or even first drafts of content.

Challenges: Ensuring that conversational AI respects user privacy, avoids bias, and provides accurate information is a top priority.

4. AI in Healthcare Content

Medical Content Generation

AI is revolutionizing healthcare content creation, from medical reports to patient education materials.

Application Examples:

Medical Reports: AI can assist doctors in generating comprehensive medical reports and recommendations.

Patient Education: AI-generated patient education materials can help individuals better understand their conditions and treatment options.

Challenges: Accuracy, data privacy, and ethical use of AI in healthcare content are critical concerns.

5. AI-Powered Personalization

Content Personalization

AI is taking personalization to the next level, providing users with content that is tailored to their individual preferences and needs.

Application Examples:

Personalized Marketing: AI can create highly personalized marketing materials, such as product recommendations, email content, and advertisements.

Education: AI-driven educational content can adapt to each student's learning pace and style, making learning more effective.

Challenges: Balancing personalization with privacy and avoiding the creation of filter bubbles are ongoing challenges.

6. AI and Data Journalism

Data-Driven Reporting

AI is helping journalists sift through massive datasets to uncover stories and present data in a more accessible manner.

Application Examples:

Data Visualization: AI can create compelling data visualizations and infographics to accompany news articles.

Investigative Journalism: AI tools can assist investigative journalists by analysing vast amounts of data quickly.

Challenges: Maintaining journalistic integrity and avoiding the dissemination of misleading or biased information are essential in AI-driven data journalism.

7. AI in Gaming Content

Enhanced Gaming Experiences

AI is transforming the gaming industry, from procedural content generation to in-game dialogue.

Application Examples:

Procedural Generation: AI can create vast, dynamic game worlds with unique content in real-time.

Adaptive Storytelling: AI-driven characters can adapt their dialogue and behaviour based on the player's actions.

Challenges: Balancing the unpredictability of AI-generated content with a coherent gaming experience is a creative challenge for developers.

8. AI and Accessibility

Inclusive Content Creation

AI is helping make content more accessible to people with disabilities, such as generating alternative text for images or translating content into sign language.

Application Examples:

Accessibility Tools: AI-driven tools can automatically generate alt text for images on websites, making content accessible to screen readers.

Sign Language Interpretation: AI can convert spoken or written content into sign language for video content or real-time communication.

Challenges: Ensuring that AI-generated accessibility features are accurate and culturally sensitive is vital.

9. AI in Creative Writing

AI as Co-Creator

AI is increasingly being used in creative writing, helping authors generate ideas, brainstorm plots, and even co-write books.

Application Examples:

pg. 158

Co-Authoring: Authors can collaborate with AI to co-write books, leveraging AI's ability to generate content at scale.

Content Inspiration: AI can provide writers with prompts and ideas, sparking creativity.

Challenges: Maintaining the authenticity and unique voice of human authors while collaborating with AI is a creative challenge.

10. AI in Content Moderation

Enhanced Moderation

AI is playing a significant role in content moderation, helping platforms identify and remove harmful or inappropriate content.

Application Examples

Hate Speech Detection: AI can automatically detect and remove hate speech from online platforms.

Child Protection: AI helps identify and remove content that involves child exploitation.

Challenges: Striking a balance between content moderation and freedom of expression is a significant ethical challenge.

11. AI-Enhanced Content Distribution

Content Delivery Optimization

AI is optimizing content distribution, ensuring that content reaches the right audience at the right time.

Application Examples:

Recommendation Systems: AI-driven recommendation algorithms can suggest content tailored to a user's preferences.

Content Scheduling: AI can determine the best times to publish content for maximum reach.

Challenges: Ensuring that AI algorithms recommend content that is diverse and avoids reinforcing biases is a challenge.

12. AI and Virtual Reality (VR)

Immersive Content

AI and VR are converging to create immersive and interactive content experiences.

Application Examples:

Immersive Storytelling: AI-generated characters and narratives can adapt to a user's choices in VR environments.

Training Simulations: AI-driven VR simulations are used for training in various fields, from medicine to aviation.

Challenges: Ensuring that AI-generated content in VR is responsive and realistic requires sophisticated technology.

13. AI in Content Localization

Global Content Reach

AI is facilitating content localization, enabling content to be easily adapted for global audiences.

Application Examples:

Automated Translation: AI can automatically translate content into multiple languages, making it accessible to a global audience.

Cultural Adaptation: AI can help ensure that content is culturally sensitive and relevant when adapted for different regions.

Challenges: Ensuring that automated translations capture the nuances and idioms of each language is a challenge.

14. AI-Generated Music and Art

Creative Expression

AI is pushing the boundaries of what is possible in music composition and visual art.

Application Examples:

Music Composition: AI can compose original music, imitating various musical styles or even creating entirely new genres.

Art Creation: AI can generate art pieces that are sold as unique digital collectibles.

Challenges: Addressing the ethical and creative implications of AI-generated art and music in the context of human creators is an ongoing debate.

15. AI-Generated Video Content

Automated Video Production

AI is entering the realm of video content creation, from scriptwriting to video editing.

Application Examples:

Scriptwriting: AI can assist in generating scripts for videos, providing ideas and even dialogue.

Video Editing: AI can automatically edit video content, enhancing visual and auditory elements.

Challenges: Ensuring that AI-generated video content aligns with the intended tone and message of the creators is a creative challenge.

16. AI in Content Verification and Fact-Checking

Ensuring Accuracy

AI is being used to verify the accuracy of content, particularly in the context of news and journalism.

Application Examples:

Fake News Detection: AI can help identify and flag potentially false or misleading news articles.

Image and Video Verification: AI can analyse the authenticity of images and videos to identify manipulation.

Challenges: Achieving high accuracy in content verification and fact-checking is a significant technological challenge.

The future of AI-generated content is a landscape of boundless possibilities and exciting developments. From GANs to conversational AI, content personalization, and immersive experiences in VR, AI is reshaping the way content is created, distributed, and consumed across various domains. As these technologies continue to evolve, addressing ethical, legal, and creative challenges will be essential to harness the full potential of AI in content generation. The world of AI-generated content is dynamic, and it promises to redefine the way we communicate, learn, entertain, and create.

Chapter 15: Case Studies and Success Stories

As we delve into the world of AI content generation, it's essential to explore case studies and success stories from various industries. This chapter presents real-world examples of how AI-driven content creation has revolutionized businesses, examines Return on Investment (ROI) analysis, shares lessons learned, and explores future strategies for leveraging AI content generation.

15.1 Success Stories from Various Industries

1. E-commerce: Enhancing Product Descriptions

Industry: E-commerce

Challenge: A major e-commerce platform sought to improve its product descriptions to boost sales and provide more comprehensive information to customers.

Solution: They employed AI content generation to create unique, informative, and SEO-friendly product descriptions. AI analysed product specifications, user reviews, and customer preferences to generate compelling content for thousands of products.

Result: The e-commerce giant experienced a significant increase in conversion rates and a 35% boost in organic search traffic. AI-driven content helped customers make informed purchasing decisions, leading to higher customer satisfaction.

2. Healthcare: Automated Medical Reports

Industry: Healthcare

Challenge: A busy medical practice was overwhelmed with manual medical report generation, which was time-consuming and prone to errors.

Solution: They integrated AI content generation to automate medical report creation. AI analysed patient data, test results, and medical histories to generate detailed reports in a fraction of the time.

Result: The practice saw a 60% reduction in report generation time, allowing medical professionals to focus on patient care. The accuracy of reports improved, reducing the risk of errors.

3. Journalism: Data-Driven Reporting

Industry: Journalism

Challenge: A news agency aimed to produce more data-driven and visually appealing news stories but faced challenges in sifting through massive datasets.

Solution: They employed AI-driven data journalism tools to analyze data, extract insights, and create compelling visualizations. AI also helped automate the creation of infographics.

Result: The agency produced data-driven stories that resonated with readers, leading to increased engagement and subscriptions. Journalists had more time for in-depth reporting, and data-driven stories became a hallmark of their brand.

4. Entertainment: Procedural Content Generation in Gaming

Industry: Gaming

Challenge: A game development studio sought to create dynamic and immersive game worlds but was constrained by manual content creation.

Solution: They integrated procedural content generation powered by AI. AI algorithms generated terrain, character behaviours, and even dialogue, making game worlds dynamic and unique for every player.

Result: The studio's games received critical acclaim for their immersive and dynamic environments. Gamers praised the unpredictability and re-playability of their titles, leading to increased sales and player retention.

15.2 ROI Analysis of AI Content Generation

Calculating the ROI

Evaluating the return on investment of AI content generation involves considering the costs of implementing AI solutions and the benefits they bring. Here's a breakdown of the ROI calculation:

Costs of Implementation: These include the expenses related to acquiring AI tools or platforms, training staff, and potential infrastructure upgrades.

Benefits: Benefits encompass various aspects, such as increased sales, reduced labor costs, improved content quality, enhanced user engagement, and better search engine rankings.

ROI Calculation: The ROI is calculated using the formula:

ROI (%) = [(Benefits - Costs) / Costs] x 100

Examples of ROI in AI Content Generation

E-commerce Platform: After investing $100,000 in AI-driven product descriptions, the platform saw a $300,000 increase in annual revenue. The ROI for this implementation would be:

ROI = [($300,000 - $100,000) / $100,000] x 100 = 200%

This means the e-commerce platform received a 200% return on their AI investment.

Medical Practice: By investing $50,000 in AI-generated medical reports, the practice saved $30,000 in labour costs and saw a 20% increase in patient referrals. The ROI calculation would be:

ROI = [($30,000 - $50,000) / $50,000] x 100 = -40%

In this case, the negative ROI indicates that the investment did not yield a positive return. However, the practice still benefited from increased efficiency and patient referrals.

News Agency: A $75,000 investment in AI-driven data journalism tools led to a 15% increase in subscriptions and a $50,000 increase in annual revenue. The ROI would be:

ROI = [($50,000 - $75,000) / $75,000] x 100 = -33.33%

Despite the negative ROI, the agency experienced revenue growth and a larger subscriber base, demonstrating the non-monetary benefits of AI content generation.

15.3 Closing Thoughts :

This chapter has provided a compelling look into the transformative power of AI across diverse industries, including e-commerce, healthcare, journalism, education, and gaming. Through a lens of real-world case studies and success stories, we've witnessed how AI has become a driving force behind innovation, efficiency, and competitive advantage.

In the realm of **e-commerce**, AI-driven personalization, recommendation engines, and chatbots have not only enhanced the customer experience but also led to substantial revenue growth. E-commerce giants have demonstrated how understanding customer behaviour, analysing data, and providing personalized recommendations can significantly impact ROI.

Healthcare, a sector with immense potential for AI, has seen remarkable developments. From early disease detection to drug discovery, AI-driven solutions have saved lives and resources. The ability to harness AI's predictive capabilities has led to better patient outcomes and more cost-effective healthcare delivery.

In **journalism**, AI has revolutionized content creation, automated fact-checking, and even identified emerging trends. It has allowed news organizations to produce quality content more efficiently while maintaining their commitment to truth and accuracy.

Education has not been left untouched by AI's transformative potential. AI-powered personalized learning platforms have enabled tailored education experiences for students, resulting in improved learning outcomes. Moreover, educators have found that AI can help automate administrative tasks, giving them more time to focus on teaching.

Gaming has seen AI play a pivotal role in creating immersive, dynamic, and challenging experiences. Game developers have harnessed AI for creating lifelike characters, adaptive gameplay, and improved player engagement. This has led to greater player satisfaction and, ultimately, increased revenue.

Finding the return on investment (ROI) for AI implementation has been a critical theme in all these industries. The success stories presented here emphasize that while AI implementation may require initial investments, the long-term gains far outweigh the costs. These gains extend beyond financial benefits and often include improved user experiences, streamlined processes, and a competitive edge.

As we conclude this chapter, it is evident that AI's potential to transform industries is not merely theoretical but a practical reality. By studying these case studies and understanding the ROI they provide, we can appreciate the tangible impact AI is having on our world. It is crucial for businesses and organizations across sectors to recognize the potential of AI, invest wisely, and continue to adapt to remain competitive in an increasingly AI-driven world. The key takeaway is that the journey to AI implementation, when guided by a clear strategy, can lead to both financial success and a positive impact on society.

Chapter 16. Typical Killer Prompts example in ChatGPT

16.1 Killer Prompt -1

Prompt for promoting an E-Book in social media.

Creating a compelling landing page for an E-Book promotion in social media is crucial for attracting and converting potential readers. Here are 10 killer prompts along with AI-generated output to guide you in this process. You may use it as appropriate for your requirement.

1. Prompt: "Craft an attention-grabbing headline for your E-Book landing page."

AI Output: "Unlock the Secrets of Success: Your Ultimate Guide to [E-Book Topic]"

2. Prompt: "Describe the key benefits of your E-Book on the landing page."

AI Output: "Discover the practical wisdom and actionable insights that [E-Book Title] offers, empowering you to [Main Benefit]."

3. Prompt: "Highlight the problem your E-Book solves."

AI Output: "[E-Book Title] is the solution to [Problem], providing you with a clear path to [Solution]."

4. Prompt: "Emphasize the unique value proposition of your E-Book."

AI Output: "What sets [E-Book Title] apart? Our E-Book offers an exclusive blend of [Unique Value Proposition]."

5. Prompt: "Explain who your E-Book is for."

AI Output: "[E-Book Title] is tailored for [Target Audience], whether you're a [Description of Audience]."

6. Prompt: "Create a compelling call-to-action (CTA) for your landing page."

AI Output: "Grab your copy of [E-Book Title] now and embark on your journey to [Desired Outcome]."

7. Prompt: "Include social proof or testimonials to build trust."

AI Output: "Read what our satisfied readers have to say about [E-Book Title]."

8. Prompt: "Outline the table of contents or key chapters of your E-Book."

AI Output: "Explore the wealth of knowledge within [E-Book Title], including chapters like 'Chapter 1: [Chapter Title]' and 'Chapter 2: [Chapter Title].'"

9. Prompt: "Provide a sneak peek or a free sample of your E-Book."

AI Output: "Get a taste of [E-Book Title] with our free sample chapter: '[Chapter Title].'"

10. Prompt: "Address objections or concerns potential readers might have."

AI Output: "Worried about [Objection]? Rest assured, [E-Book Title] equips you with the tools to overcome any challenge."

These prompts and their AI-generated outputs serve as a foundation for a compelling landing page that will engage your audience and encourage them to take action, whether it's downloading or purchasing your E-Book. Remember to further customize and optimize the content for your specific E-Book and target audience.

16.2 Killer Prompt-2

Prompt for creating a landing page in Face Book for promoting your Book " Unveiling India: A 30-day Journey of Discovery"

Prompt :

Create a face book ad for me for promotion of my E-Book " Unveiling India: A 30-day Journey of Discovery" that has Detailed day-wise itinerary from arrival to departure. (Day-1 to Day-30 explained along with hash tags **Prompt** :

AI Output :

Explore India Like Never Before! IN

Embark on a 30-Day Journey of Discovery with "Unveiling India" - Your Ultimate Guide to Experiencing the Heart of India.

Are you ready to unravel the secrets of India's rich culture, history, and landscapes? This E-Book is your passport to a once-in-a-lifetime adventure!

Discover India's Hidden Treasures:

Detailed Day-wise Itinerary from Day 1 to Day 30

Explore Iconic Landmarks

Savor Authentic Indian Cuisine

Immerse in Festivals and Traditions

Capture Unforgettable Moments

Your Itinerary Includes:

* Day 1: Arrival in Delhi - #DelhiDiaries

* Day 5: Taj Mahal in Agra - #TajMahalMagic

* Day 10: Jaipur's Royal Heritage - #PinkCityPalace

* Day 20: Mystical Varanasi - #GangesGlow

* Day 30: Departure from Mumbai - #IncredibleIndia

Don't miss out on the adventure of a lifetime! Grab your copy now and let's embark on a journey together.

Get Your E-Book Here: [Link to Your E-Book]

🎁 BONUS: Exclusive Travel Tips & Packing Guide Included!

Join fellow adventurers, share your experiences, and use #UnveilingIndiaEbook to connect with like-minded explorers. Let's make this journey unforgettable! 📷 🌍 ✨

💧 Unveil India's Magic Today! 💧

16.3 Killer Prompt-3

Prompt for creating an E-Book

Here is an effective prompt for creating a Table of Contents for your E-Book titled "How to Invest and Succeed in Crypto Business":

Step-1 : In Step -1 you need to write a prompt for crating a Table of Content for your E-Book.

Prompt-1 : "Craft a comprehensive Table of Contents for your E-Book 'How to Invest and Succeed in Crypto Business' that outlines the key chapters and sections, providing readers with a clear roadmap of the valuable insights and knowledge they will gain from the book."

AI Output :

pg. 179

Certainly, here's a comprehensive Table of Contents for your E-Book titled "How to Invest and Succeed in Crypto Business." This outlines the key chapters and sections, providing readers with a clear roadmap of the valuable insights and knowledge they will gain from the book:

Table of Contents

Introduction

1. Understanding the Crypto Landscape

- What Is Cryptocurrency?

- A Brief History of Cryptocurrency

- The Promise of Blockchain Technology

- Types of Cryptocurrencies

2. Getting Started in Crypto

- Setting Your Investment Goals

- Creating a Cryptocurrency Wallet

- Choosing the Right Cryptocurrency Exchange

- Ensuring Security and Safety

3. Investment Strategies in Cryptocurrency

- Learning from Mistakes

- Building a Cryptocurrency Portfolio

- Continuing Your Crypto Journey

Appendix

11. Glossary of Crypto Terms

- A Handy Reference Guide

12. Recommended Resources

- Books, Websites, and Communities

By providing this comprehensive Table of Contents, your readers will have a clear roadmap of the valuable insights and knowledge they can expect to gain from your E-Book on investing and succeeding in the crypto business.

Step-2 : In Step -2 you need to write a prompt for asking AI to describe each section in detail:

Prompt : Elaborate and describe Chapter-1 in detail giving real life examples in not less than 5 pages.

Prompt : Elaborate and describe Chapter-2 in detail giving real life examples in not less than 5 pages.

This will continue for all the 10 Chapters

16.4 Conclusion / Recommendation:

Your Journey to AI Content Mastery.

Dear Readers,

As we reach the final chapter of "Mastering the Art of Prompt Engineering with ChatGPT: Tricks for framing Killer Prompts in 2023," you've embarked on a transformative odyssey through the world of AI content generation. This isn't just a book; it's your passport to the future. Let's wrap up this journey with a resounding conclusion and a strong recommendation for those who seek to master AI content creation.

Why "Mastering the Art of Prompt Engineering" is a Must-Read:

A Paradigm Shift in Content Creation: In the digital age of 2023, traditional content generation methods are rapidly evolving. This E-Book is your guide to embracing the transformative power of ChatGPT and staying ahead in the game.

Creative Empowerment: You've discovered how to turn AI into your creative ally, crafting content that's engaging, informative, and persuasive. The strategies and techniques shared within these pages empower you to harness the AI's creative potential fully.

Adapt to the Changing Landscape: The AI landscape is in constant flux, but this E-Book equips you with the knowledge and tools to adapt, innovate, and thrive in a dynamic content creation environment.

Practical, Actionable Insights: It's not just about theory; you've learned practical implementation. From crafting prompts to refining outputs, you've gained hands-on experience, making you ready to apply your knowledge immediately.

Our Recommendation: "Unlock the Power of AI Content Generation**

In light of your journey through this E-Book, we strongly recommend taking the next step toward mastering AI content generation. The future of content creation is inextricably linked with AI, and your investment in this knowledge is an investment in your creative future.

How to Get Started:

1. **Apply What You've Learned**: Take the concepts, strategies, and techniques from this E-Book and apply them to your projects. Start small, and gradually integrate AI content generation into your workflow. Try creating prompts based on your requirement and fine tune the prompts as long as you get the result they way you want.

2. **Collaborate and Learn**: Join a community of like-minded individuals who are navigating the AI content landscape. Share your experiences, learn from others, and stay updated on the latest trends and developments.

3. **Stay Informed:** The world of AI is ever-changing. Keep yourself updated with the latest advancements, tools, and best practices to ensure that you remain at the forefront of AI content generation.

4. **Experiment and Innovate**: Don't be afraid to experiment. Innovation often comes from trying new things, pushing the boundaries, and thinking creatively.

Your Path to the Future Begins Here:

pg. 186

In these pages, you've acquired the keys to unlock your creative potential and master the art and science of AI content generation. The future is waiting for those who are willing to embrace change and adapt to new possibilities. Don't miss this opportunity to shape the content landscape of 2023 and beyond.

🚀 Get Your Copy Today !!!!

A Closing Note

Thank you for choosing this book. Our creation gets improved with your opinions. Would be grateful for your valuable feedback!

Visit the Authors Page below to discover our books collection !!!!!

"https://www.amazon.com/author/prabhakarv

For AI enthusiasts who want to stand ahead in AI technology.

Visit our website :

https://promthub.blogspot.com/

For Bloggers who want to turn as Pro Blogger.

https://bloglikeapro.in

www.ingramcontent.com/pod-product-compliance
Lightning Source LLC
Chambersburg PA
CBHW050515160726
48003CB00001B/308